LANGUAGE AND LIT

Dorothy S. Strickland,
Celia Genishi and Donna E. Al

ADVISORY BOARD: *Richard Allington, Kathryn.*
Anne Haas Dyson, Carole Edelsky, Mary Juzwik, Susan Lytle, Django Paris, Timothy Shanahan

continued

For volumes in the NCRLL Collection (edited by JoBeth Allen and Donna E. Alvermann) and the Practitioners Bookshelf Series
(edited by Celia Genishi and Donna E. Alvermann), as well as other titles in this series, please visit www.tcpress.com.

ARTS INTEGRATION IN DIVERSE K–5 CLASSROOMS

Cultivating Literacy Skills and Conceptual Understanding

Liane Brouillette

TEACHERS COLLEGE PRESS

TEACHERS COLLEGE | COLUMBIA UNIVERSITY
NEW YORK AND LONDON

Published by Teachers College Press, 1234 Amsterdam Avenue, New York, NY 10027

Cover photo by: Klaus Vedfelt / Getty Images.

Library of Congress Cataloging-in-Publication Data is available at loc.gov

Names: Brouillette, Liane, 1947– author.
Title: Arts integration in diverse K-5 classrooms : cultivating literacy skills and conceptual understanding / Liane Brouillette.
Description: New York, NY : Teachers College Press, [2019] | Series: Language and literacy series | Includes bibliographical references and index.
Identifiers: LCCN 2019011056
ISBN 9780807761571 (pbk. : alk. paper)
ISBN 9780807761823 (hardcover : alk. paper)
ISBN 9780807777985 (ebook)
Subjects: LCSH: Language arts (Elementary) | Language arts (Elementary)–Curricula. | Arts–Study and teaching (Elementary) | Arts–Study and teaching (Elementary)–Curricula. | Arts in education. | Concept learning–Study and teaching (Elementary)

Classification: LCC LB1575.8 .B75 2019 | DDC 372.6–dc23
LC record available at https://lccn.loc.gov/2019011056

ISBN 978-0-8077-6157-1 (paper)
ISBN 978-0-8077-6182-3 (hardcover)
ISBN 978-0-8077-7798-5 (ebook)

Printed on acid-free paper
Manufactured in the United States of America

Contents

Deepening Understanding Through Arts Integration

> On a rainy day, 1st-graders giggle and dance in an empty cafeteria. In time to the music, they reach up high, bend down low, wiggle, then freeze; they take a step forward, then one backward. The children mimic their teacher in jumping for joy, then letting their shoulders slump as if in sadness. Through dance, the class is learning about binary opposites.

The lesson described above closely aligns with the Common Core State Standards in English language arts for 1st grade (CCSS.ELA-LITERA-CY.L.1.5). Yet, this is also a standards-based dance lesson. Exploring instances of overlap between the visual and performing arts and the language arts standards can be both valuable and fun. This book discusses many such intersections, showing how teachers have made use of these commonalities to introduce literacy concepts in engaging ways and rehearse reading skills by integrating them into visual and performing arts lessons.

The challenge this book takes on in the following pages is to identify areas in a crowded K–5 curriculum where arts integration can both spark genuine aesthetic experiences and assist students in mastering demanding literacy skills. As Parsons (1992) pointed out, the objective for students is to (1) learn to discuss what is hard to see and (2) find ways to see what is hard to say. Over time aesthetic and linguistic means of comprehension can interact so as to provide a more complete picture of the world, with insights derived from both language and the arts.

UNDERSTANDING ARTS INTEGRATION

As Elliot Eisner (1982, 2002) observed, humans learn by forming representations of their experiences. Children's ability to visualize a state of affairs—whether encountered through art or in real life—allows them to

1

stabilize an image in their mind so they can remember it. This enables them to play out possible responses to similar situations in their imagination, so they can anticipate the consequences of their actions. For adults, this process can be abstract and internal; but for children, concrete representation is often critical for understanding (Inhelder & Piaget, 1958). The visual and performing arts can therefore provide appealing and effective vehicles to help children represent concepts to themselves in K–5 classrooms and in daily life.

Yet, arriving at a shared definition of *arts integration* can be a challenge. Therefore, this book uses the definition of arts integration developed by the John F. Kennedy Center for the Performing Arts:

> Arts integration is an approach to teaching in which students construct and demonstrate understanding through an art form. Students engage in a creative process which connects an art form to another subject area and meets evolving objectives in both. (Silverstein & Layne, 2010)

Opened in 1971, the Kennedy Center serves as a national cultural center for the United States in Washington, DC. In addition to offering a wide array of performances, it has become a nexus for arts education. Yet, in the center's initial years, the quality of arts integration provided by teachers in classrooms varied widely. So, the Kennedy Center began a process of clarifying the key ideas at the foundation of its work.

Part of the process involved exploring what it means to engage in a creative process by examining connections between an art form and another content area. Educators inquired: What is it like to pursue dual learning objectives, with the goal of gaining a greater understanding of both? For example, 2nd-graders might act out a scene from a story to obtain deeper insight into why the characters made certain choices; but these students also meet objectives in theater (understanding characterization or describing the action and expressions). Fifth-graders reading about the American Revolution may, in order to arrive at a better understanding of the conflicting perceptions of the rebels and the redcoats, learn songs of the colonial rebels as well as ones sung by the English soldiers. At the same time, students learn about the cultural and historical background of tunes still widely played every Fourth of July.

Pathway to Literacy

For adults who have become fluent readers, the world overflows with readily available knowledge. Newspapers, road signs, novels, and the Internet lie open to their glance. As these citizens vote, pay taxes, consult maps, or send emails, they give hardly a thought to what it would be like if the letters and numbers that form a crucial part of their daily life were incomprehensible. Yet, even in industrialized nations, large numbers of people never achieve fluent literacy.

When researchers conducted the first U.S. National Adult Literacy Survey in 1992 (Kirsch, Jungeblut, Jenkins, & Kolstad, 1993), it revealed that the literacy of about 40 million adults was so limited that they could understand only the simplest of written instructions. A 2003 follow-up study showed no significant change in the numbers. More recently, the United States has participated in the Programme for the International Assessment of Adult Competencies (PIAAC), developed under the auspices of the Organisation for Economic Cooperation and Development (OECD). In 2012, the PIAAC showed that the statistics on skills of adults in the United States had remained relatively unchanged in the decade following the previous PIAAC report, while other nations had been showing improvements, especially among adults with low basic skills (OECD, 2013).

Since 1992, states and the federal government have increasingly put pressure on schools to make sure that all students learn basic academic skills. The reasons are largely economic; in an increasingly technological era, basic academic skills are necessary for the economic mobility of individuals and the quality of the labor force. In 2012, for example, the poverty rate was only 2% among adults who graduated from high school, worked full-time, and delayed having children until they were married and out of their teenage years (Sawhill & Rodrigue, 2015). Of course, myriad factors affect a student's transition into adulthood. The one factor that an elected government can easily influence, however, is the public schools.

In recent decades, adoption of state standards for—and assessment of—student learning has forced schools to become more instrumental, goal-oriented organizations (Elmore, 2000). The passage of the No Child Left Behind Act (NCLB) of 2001 challenged schools to prevent practically all failures, at least in the pivotal fields of language arts and mathematics (Bellamy, Crawford, Marshall, & Coulter, 2005). Although the standardized assessments through which student progress is measured continue to be debated, the expectation that every child will achieve at every grade level has reshaped the social context of schools. The new assessments benchmarked to the Common Core State Standards also emphasize the expectation that, by high school graduation, all students should be college or career ready. But is there a cost to this narrow, specialized focus?

Drawbacks to Standardized Testing

Powerful arguments can be made for the inclusion of the visual and performing arts in the K–12 curriculum as independent disciplines. Yet, too often, arts instruction has been crowded out of elementary schools by rising pressure to improve students' performance on standardized tests in language arts and mathematics. As will be discussed later, this has an ironic dimension, especially in schools that serve large numbers of children who speak a language other than English at home. These children need support as they learn to speak better English if they are to become fluent in that language; they could benefit greatly from multimodal learning that incorporates the arts.

If used wisely, standardized tests can provide teachers guidance as to which curricular options work best. The problem is that widespread misconceptions about what standardized tests can do has in recent years led to an unnecessary narrowing of the curriculum. So what happened? As Daniel Koretz (2017) explained, political polls offer a helpful analogy. In national and state elections, there are far too many voters for pollsters to survey them all. The pollsters' solution is to survey a small number of potential voters who are chosen to be representative of the voting public. The results of a poll are of value only to the extent that they provide a good prediction of the behavior of all the voters never contacted.

Standardized achievement tests resemble polls in that educators typically use them to estimate mastery of a large area of the curriculum, such as algebra or language arts. There is insufficient time to test whether students have mastered all of the knowledge and skills in a broad content area. So the authors of a test select a small sample of the larger area of study and use it to project how students would have performed if tested on everything. Just as pollsters sample a small number of people who represent the whole population of voters, the authors of tests use a small sample of content to represent an entire area of study. Most of the content area remains untested, however, just as pollsters never contact most voters.

Just as pollsters find it easier to reach voters who have listed home phones and are agreeable to being interviewed, the authors of standardized tests find some areas of the curriculum—such as factual knowledge—easier to test (Koretz, 2017). Other important skills, like analytical thinking and problem solving, are much more difficult to assess and are tested less often. In addition, the behavior of school personnel who are under pressure to raise test scores can undermine the effectiveness of tests. Because only a small portion of a content area like language arts can be tested, educational consultants have discovered they can make considerable money by analyzing high-stakes tests to predict which parts of the curriculum are likely to be included on future tests. This allows the consultants to coach teachers in struggling schools on elements of the curriculum to focus on and what they can skip without hurting students' test results.

This is why, despite the United States' placing an extreme emphasis on standardized testing in recent years, students' performance on the National Assessment of Educational Progress (NAEP) and international assessments like the OECD's Programme for International Student Assessment (PISA) has continued to be significantly below that of the top-performing nations. The nature of standardized tests is such that they cannot bear the burden that has been put on them. When accountability pressures make a test score more important than the learning it represents, the prospect of "gaming" the tests becomes inviting. That is why, when a new standardized test is introduced, test scores drop. In a few years, however, test scores rise again. Some observers will claim that this rise is evidence of increased learning. But to an objective analyst, NAEP and PISA scores reveal the illusory character of these gains over time.

The tragedy is that language arts and mathematics mastery—targeted for improvement by the No Child Left Behind legislation and the Common Core State Standards—has suffered from an overemphasis on testing. When accountability pressures reach such a point that test scores become an end in themselves, learning is undermined. This is not an argument against sensible use of standardized tests, but their limitations must be recognized. Tests must not be allowed to distort the school curriculum in unhealthy ways.

BENEFITS OF COMPREHENSIVE EDUCATION

> It is not enough to teach man a specialty. . . . Otherwise he—with his specialized knowledge—more closely resembles a well-trained dog than a harmoniously developed person. He must learn to understand the motives of human beings, their illusions and their sufferings in order to acquire a proper relationship to individual fellow men and to the community.
>
> These precious things are conveyed to the younger generation through personal contact with those who teach. —*Albert Einstein* (Fine, 1952)

Einstein's strong opinions were rooted in personal experience. Despite his transformative impact on 20th-century science, Albert Einstein did not follow a linear path to success. When he was 15, his parents moved to Italy for work, leaving him to stay in a boardinghouse while finishing high school. More interested in how things worked than in studying for examinations, he eventually ran away to join his parents. But because he was a high school dropout, his prospects were not promising. Even though Einstein had failed the entrance exam, the Swiss Federal Institute of Technology accepted him because of his exceptional math test scores. After he graduated, he had trouble finding a job. His father died thinking his son a failure (Kaku, 2017).

What was going on? Although it is easy to stereotype "high school dropouts," there are many types of setbacks that might interrupt a student's schooling. For the Einstein family, as for many others, the setback was financial. Health problems, bullying, or inadequate schooling in early grades may also play a role for students who drop out. Lack of engagement with a one-size-fits-all school curriculum is frequently part of the problem. Could more exposure to visual and performing arts experiences boost student engagement? For Einstein, it did. Chapter 7 discusses the role that tacit knowledge, which is nourished by exposure to the arts, plays in human understanding. Chapter 8 explores the role of executive function, which can be strengthened by arts activities.

Einstein did not fit the traditional conception of a scientist. He once asserted that if he had not been a scientist, he would have been a musician. "Life without playing music is inconceivable for me. I live my daydreams in music. I see my life in terms of music. . . . I get most joy in life out of music" (Foster, 2005, p. 1). Having begun violin lessons at the age of 6, Einstein as a 13-year-old fell in love with Mozart. From then on, Einstein's violin was his constant companion. His wife Elsa later wrote the following observation: "Music helps him when he is thinking of his theories. He goes to his study, comes back, strikes a few chords on the piano, jots something down, returns to his study" (Foster, 2005, p. 1).

In his own unique way, Einstein had reached the objective that Parsons (1992) later pointed to. Einstein had found a way to use musical exploration to help him "see"—or envision—scientific phenomena that had been hard to discuss. Part of Einstein's genius lay in his ability to arrive at the core of problems in physics through thought experiments, such as envisioning what it would be like to chase a beam of light (leading him to his theory of special relativity) and imagining riding an elevator in free fall (convincing him that gravity and acceleration are one and the same). As a result of these experiments—carried out only in his mind—he was able to explain in his writings various phenomena that were otherwise difficult to see.

Like the children Eisner (1982, 2002) observed, contemporary human beings learn by forming representations of their experiences. Einstein's thought experiments let him create mental representations that gave him a grasp on the conflicts he felt he needed to explore. Stabilizing an image of a set of circumstances in his mind enabled him to investigate it. Playing out the possible consequences of changes in that situation in his imagination allowed him to anticipate the effects.

Why Einstein's Experiences Are Relevant Today

Metaphorically speaking, human beings drink in the world through their eyes. Although absorbing images is a largely passive process, we have to work harder to make sense of words. So on the Internet, where people can freely choose how they prefer to receive information, visual platforms like Facebook, Pinterest, Instagram, and Snapchat are popular. Nonetheless, most of that content stays in working memory for only a matter of seconds before it is forgotten. The same can be said for much of what people observe when walking down the street. Visual input means nothing unless individuals engage with it, signaling to their brains that an image is worth remembering.

Yet, as Einstein's thought experiments showed, visual images can play a crucial role by providing people with an initial grasp of a situation, which they can then build upon. Drama can perform a similar role. In classroom drama activities, children use their bodies and voices to dramatize the actions of characters in a story. In this way, they touch, see, and experience the meaning of words in the text. As children continue to dramatize stories, these experiences can support their development of a stronger, more direct pathway from decontextualized language on a page to comprehension (Mages, 2006). This is hardly a new discovery for educators. Picture books prominently figure in every kindergarten and 1st-grade classroom, helping children visualize what is described.

Use of classroom drama in the primary grades, however, has dropped significantly since passage of the No Child Left Behind Act of 2001 (Gara, Brouillette, & Farkas, 2018). Although the Every Student Succeeds Act of 2015 has taken the place of No Child Left Behind, both laws share the goal of ensuring that—at the very least—all students master the basic skills of reading and mathematics. The assumption has been that focusing on these two pivotal skills would ease the discovery of highly reliable teaching methods that would enable all students to achieve basic levels of proficiency. The expectation was if that happened, the next step would be the creation of equally effective instructional strategies in content areas like science, history, and the arts. But reliable teaching methods that aid all students in all contexts have yet to be found, even for the targeted disciplines of reading and math (Bryk, Gomez, Grunow, & LeMahieu, 2015).

In 2011, the President's Committee on the Arts and the Humanities (PCAH) suggested a new strategy for encouraging school improvement. In a report titled *Reinvesting in Arts Education: Winning America's Future Through Creative Schools*, the committee described the strong and consistent links that researchers have found between a high-quality arts education and a wide range of positive academic outcomes. The report argued for putting greater emphasis on arts integration by strengthening teacher preparation and professional development. Critical areas in which the visual and performing arts have the potential to contribute to the broader life and academic success of K–12 students were identified. These areas included:

- Increased student academic achievement in language arts and the development of effective content area literacy curricula in mathematics, science, and social studies;
- Student motivation and engagement, leading to improved attendance and persistence; and
- Support for social competencies, including collaboration and teamwork skills, social tolerance, and self-confidence (President's Committee on the Arts and the Humanities, 2011).

This book follows up on these suggestions, focusing on how arts integration can boost student performance, with an emphasis on two key aspects of literacy: (1) meaning-making and (2) effective expression. *Meaning-making* is the central purpose for listening, speaking, interacting with text, producing text, and participating in discussions. *Effective expression* is the result of students learning to communicate well, as speakers and writers. Chapters 2, 3, and 4 are devoted to a discussion of meaning-making in connection with oral communication and narrative and informational texts. Chapters 5, 6, and 7 focus on effective speaking, narrative writing, and expository writing. In the conclusion, Chapter 8 looks at the development of social–emotional skills and executive function. Chapter 9 puts the previous chapters in a broader perspective.

Boosting Achievement Through Integration

During the NCLB era, a diminished focus on non-tested subjects like the visual and performing arts resulted in many novice teachers receiving little preparation in arts integration. Even in a tested subject like language arts, reading and writing skills received more attention than speaking and listening skills. So, although the importance of listening and speaking skills is recognized in the Common Core standards, many teachers feel ill-prepared to address the new emphasis on oral language skills. Yet, the K–5 theater curriculum has much in common with the speaking and listening aspects of language arts and can provide teachers with a wealth of engaging performing arts tools and strategies for fostering oral language development.

Performing arts activities such as drama and dance treat expressive communication as social interactions. Participants take cues from other participants and react to them, constructing and conveying meaning. Therefore, students with less developed language abilities—including English learners and struggling readers—can jointly construct language and meaning with their peers, performing at a higher level than otherwise would be possible. Students with greater language abilities can help model such communication and mediate the interaction for students with lower language abilities, thereby facilitating comprehension. Schwartz,

Bransford, and Sears (2005) argued that effective learning for people of any age requires a balance between (1) well-learned routines that provide efficiency and (2) opportunities for innovation that involve play and social interaction, allowing for new insights to emerge. As the Standards for the English Language Arts state, "We learn language not simply for the sake of learning language; we learn it to make sense of the world around us and to communicate our understandings with others" (International Reading Association & National Council of Teachers of English, 1996, p. 14).

Both written language and the visual and performing arts can serve as vehicles for giving thought an external form, enabling people to more carefully inspect, revise, and extend their ideas. Helping students acquire such tools and become fluent in their use is a central purpose of this book. As this book investigates the contribution that arts integration can make to varied aspects of the literacy curriculum, we will look at research on the nature of the cognitive tools students use to express themselves, at experimental studies that explore successful arts-based interventions, and at what standardized tests and national databases reveal about the impact that educational policy—along with local instructional decisions—has had on student learning.

Supporting Healthy Literacy Development

Providing K–5 students with an opportunity to construct and demonstrate understanding through an art form gives children who still learn best through sensory experience an element of the lesson that can help them create vivid mental representations of what they just learned. This not only holds true for kindergartners and 1st-graders but also for 3rd-graders just learning to write their own stories and 5th-graders trying to make meaning from complex texts. Without detracting from the rigor of a demanding curriculum, arts integration lets students engage with ideas at their own developmental level. Simultaneously, it preserves the sense of adventure and fun that is the rightful inheritance of children.

Each art form has its own contribution to make, according to researchers: Music has been found to strengthen academic performance and phonological skills. Classroom drama augments verbal skills, and some studies have shown that drama classes enhance empathy, perspective taking, and the ability to regulate emotion. The collaborative nature of theater can help students work together more effectively and foster a sense of community. Well-designed visual arts classes foster "studio habits of mind": developing a sense of craft, persisting with tasks, engaging, envisioning, expressing, observing, reflecting, exploring, and interacting with other artists. Dance, like team sports, provides a means for students to improve physical fitness, self-regulation, and their sense of teamwork. If taught with these goals in mind, dance can enhance body awareness while providing an effective forum for lessons about good health and nutrition.

The next seven chapters describe arts integration strategies, along with developmental factors that make these strategies helpful at certain ages or when paired with a specific academic content list of online resources, sample lesson plans, videos, and instructional materials that teachers may use is available at: sites.uci.edu/educ104donline/.

CHAPTER 2

Making Meaning Through Verbal Interaction

Laying the Foundation for Literacy

"Actors, five-point position, please!"

The kindergartners jumped to attention, standing with hands at their sides, heads high, feet together, smiling at the teaching artist who had been working closely with their classroom teacher on arts integration activities. Most of the children had limited English skills, yet they easily followed along because the teaching artist provided a demonstration as he spoke:

"I am going to read a story about a bear hunt. There are lots of sounds we can make to tell the story. I need you to help me create some sounds for the *setting* of the story. But first let's practice making some sound effects of our own."

He began to pat his legs gently to represent a light rain; then he patted stronger to suggest heavy rain. He asked the students to imitate him. Twenty pairs of hands patted their legs, creating a classroom rainstorm.

Now it was time for the bear hunt.[1]

In a soft voice, the teaching artist began his epic tale, "Going on a bear hunt." Then he switched to a loud voice: "Going to catch a big one!" Using a call-and-response pattern, the teaching artist encouraged the children to mimic his words and dynamics. As they continued with the poem, he showed them how to insert their own sounds to create the changing setting as the narrator described swishy grass, gooey mud, tall trees, a deep river, and a dark cave.

---

1. Classroom videos and lesson plan for a longer version of this lesson are available online at: http://sltes.uci.edu/class/kindergarten/theater-kindergarten/kindergarten-theater-lesson-2/

THE CRITICAL IMPORTANCE OF ORAL LANGUAGE DEVELOPMENT

Storytelling activities of this kind are simple, yet engaging; they provide native English speakers as well as English language learners (ELLs) a rich opportunity for vocabulary development. Such lessons complement what many teachers are already doing in their classrooms. The lessons are close-ly related to the Common Core standards for K–2 English language arts (ELA), specifically in speaking and listening. The first ELA speaking and listening standard for each of these grade levels calls for students "to par-ticipate in collaborative conversations with diverse partners [and] with peers and adults in small and larger groups" (www.corestandards.org/ELA-Literacy/SL).

Through dramatization and movement, children learn to engage in call-and-response communication with one another and their teachers. Drama lessons provide students the opportunity to practice pronuncia-tion, tone, and gestures, helping them learn to "speak audibly and express thoughts, feelings, and ideas clearly," as the Common Core standards for kindergarten put it. After the teaching artist leaves, the classroom teacher uses similar techniques to teach voice projection.

The classroom teacher later recalled the teaching artist's techniques:

> He talked about voice projection and I still use that. I call it 'loud and proud.' . . . So, I bring that into my lessons when we're having a discus-sion. I'll be like, "Okay, Michelle, I'm going to call on you; give it to me loud and proud."

Another classroom teacher added the following:

> In theater, a lot of vocabulary words required using your imagination, using expression. So that kind of lent itself to when you read a book and there's an exclamation mark. You're not going to read it like you're normally talking. You're going to read like you're excited because you're going to the park or swimming. So, let's change your voice. In Goldilocks, when she saw the bears, she didn't say, "Oh, my." She said, "Oh, *my*!"

Yet, pressures associated with standardized testing have discouraged many teachers from using arts-based activities as strategies for teaching lit-eracy skills. In recent decades, the early elementary curriculum has been transformed. The changes are most noticeable in kindergarten, which has been converted from a playful interlude focused on children's social, emotional, and moral development to the beginning of serious academ-ic instruction (Russell, 2011). First and 2nd grade have similarly become more academic. Scholars have argued that the backward mapping of expectations from standardized tests has warped practice (Bassok, Latham, & Rorem, 2016; Graue, 2009), causing even the kindergarten curriculum to become one-sidedly focused on teaching academic content.

How Children Learn Language

Before beginning to talk, an infant will spontaneously communicate by crying in pain, laughing with joy, and pointing at desired objects. This works well as long as the child's needs are simple. But sometimes a caregiver is preoccupied or does not understand. Then the child feels frustrated and looks for other ways to get the message across. Through interactions with caregivers, the infant learns that the words spoken by adults serve as signals. By experimenting with the language behaviors used by parents and siblings, the child gradually learns how to communicate his or her desires using words. Social interaction thus plays a pivotal role in language development, as does the child's impulse to communicate.

When children enter kindergarten, they are still in the process of mastering their home language by means of social interaction. That means that isolating primary-grade students at their desks for much of the day could slow their progress in learning language. Think of children of this age playing on their own. Dramatic play—whether playing house or pretending to be mythic heroes—comes naturally to young children and serves a crucial role in their construction of meaning (Piaget, 1962). Teachers can put this sense of dramatic narrative to use in literacy lessons by having children act out stories or discuss plot, character, and themes.

Such activities are especially valuable for English language learners. Classroom drama allows them to inject their own cultural understanding into the story, using alternative modes of communication so they can engage in a meaningful dialogue despite their limited English vocabulary (Greenfader & Brouillette, 2013). When children improvise scenes from stories, they immediately bring their own experiences to bear. By dramatizing stories, students come to better understand the plot and the feelings of the characters, even if they do not initially comprehend all the words.

Mages (2006) proposed a causal model to explain the impact that creative drama has been shown to have on literacy and language development. By using their bodies and voices to dramatize the characters' words and actions, children gain a sense of how interactions among the various personalities shaped the events described in the story. "In this way they can touch, see, and experience the meaning of the words in the text" (Mages, 2006, p. 335). As children continue to dramatize stories, they build a stronger more direct pathway from the decontextualized language on the page to comprehension of what the words mean. Harris (2000) explained, "the role player projects him- or herself into the make-believe situation faced by the protagonist" (p. 36). Having fed the make-believe situation into their own knowledge base, children arrive at feelings and utterances appropriate for the role. By fully engaging their imaginations, children increase their ability to mentally simulate the events, characters, and nuances of a story. As the children become better able to project themselves into the make-believe world of a narrative, they eventually approach a point where dramatization may no longer be needed for comprehension.

Many early elementary school teachers intuitively sense that oral language is important. Scores of researchers have cited the importance of practicing oral language skills at a young age for monolingual or bilingual literacy development (August & Shanahan, 2006). At the K–2 grade level, the Common Core speaking and listening standards emphasize the need for a rich verbal dialogue between students and with adults. Yet, preliminary research on the implementation of the CCSS indicates that the teacher preparation and professional development required to fully realize it may be lacking (McLaughlin, Glaab, & Carrasco, 2014). Other research suggests that early elementary teachers of ELLs lack the training and preparation to successfully meet students' needs (Samson & Lesaux, 2015).

Helping Children Dramatize Stories

How might a teacher utilize classroom drama to enable children in the primary grades to touch, see, and experience the meaning of the words in a story? At the beginning of this chapter, we saw a teaching artist use sound effects to help kindergartners imagine what it was like to go hiking through a wild countryside. Now, we will look at how the same teaching artist used drama to help children project themselves into a make-believe situation faced by characters in a story.[2] After a vocal and physical warm-up, he taught them the vocabulary words *actor* (a human being who plays a role), *character* (a role an actor plays), and *setting* (where the story takes place). Sitting in a circle with the children, he read the story of "Goldilocks and the Three Bears," pausing afterward to discuss the four characters, the setting, and the children's roles as actors. Then they re-enacted the story, with each child given something simple and specific to do.

To provide as many children as possible a chance to take part, the teaching artist assigned roughly a third of the class to play Papa Bear, another third of the class to serve as Mama Bear, and the remaining third of the class to act as Baby Bear, with one girl playing Goldilocks. He worked with the Papa Bears so they could imagine how a bear might growl and scowl after discovering that someone had slept in his bed. Then he had the Mama Bears stand up and envision the motions of a sassy, no-nonsense bear who

2. Video: http://sites.uci.edu/class/kindergarten/theater-kindergarten/kindergarten-theater-lesson-4/

just discovered that someone had slept in her bed. Next, he worked with the Baby Bears on what they will say when they discover Goldilocks is sleeping in their bed. After this, he coached Goldilocks to knock on the door, listen for footsteps, shrug, and let herself in when no one arrives to answer her knock. The story was read again, with pauses for the child actors to say their lines. Adults prompted the actors, as needed, to speak their lines clearly, with emotion.

Following the re-enactment, the teaching artist congratulated the group. Then he initiated a quick review, asking the class, "What do you call yourself when you stand up and create the Papa Bear or the Mama Bear? What word did we learn for the role an actor creates? What is the word that describes where the story takes place?" Then he had them pat themselves on the back.

A classroom teacher could easily lead this activity, without a teaching artist. The lesson's objective is to build students' listening and responding skills by (1) showing how actors use their tools to portray characters in a story and (2) having children vividly imagine and bring to life specific characters. Because multiple children played the same role, the whole class shared in the experience. This approach generally works well with young children, though some youngsters may feel shy when singled out.

SUPPORTING ENGLISH LANGUAGE LEARNERS

Many classroom teachers do not feel—and are not—adequately prepared to instruct young ELLs (Elfers & Stritikus, 2013; National Education Association, 2008). Therefore, determining *how* to effectively assist educators in providing young ELLs with needed English language skills to meet the CCSS has become a pressing matter. Fortunately, many classroom activities helpful to English learners also benefit native English speakers. A report summarizing research on early literacy, published by the National Governors Association, pointed out where earlier attempts to boost literacy skills fell short:

> Many state policies and practices emphasize mechanics of reading (for example, matching letters to sounds and sounding out whole words) at the expense of other skills. However, proficiency requires more, notably development of oral language skills, an expanding vocabulary, the ability to comprehend what is read, and a rich understanding of real-world concepts and subject matter. (National Governors Association, 2013, p. 3)

When early elementary school teachers integrate into the classroom lineup arts lessons that emphasize verbal interaction and mimic how youngsters learn their home language, these educators build a foundation for literacy. Providing close-up examples of how this process can work was the repertoire of the Teaching Artist Project (TAP), an arts-based professional development project for educators carried out in K–2 classrooms at 15 San Diego public schools that served diverse populations from 2010 to 2014. Each teacher co-taught weekly arts integration lessons with a teaching artist. The lesson described above was drawn from the TAP program. A majority of teachers involved found the intervention beneficial (Greenfader & Brouillette, 2013) and cited improvements in student literacy skills, teachers' comfort levels when teaching the arts, and the engagement of students, especially ELLs. One teacher commented:

> The children who had been in kindergarten last year and are now my 1st-graders moved two levels [on the California language development test]. Two full levels!

Although teachers indicated that ELLs benefited most from the TAP program, they affirmed that native English speakers also profited from its focus on oral language. Teachers described direct and indirect effects of the arts activities on participants. At the individual level, teachers credited multisensory activity (pairing gesture and language, such as when Papa Bear growled and scowled after discovering that someone had slept in his bed), rhythm and syllable practice, and increased engagement as having a direct impact on children's language skills. Beyond this, many teachers described a shift in the classroom climate outside the arts lessons. In interviews, teachers commented that the arts activities created an enhanced sense of community in the classroom, which helped address behavioral concerns. (Lesson plans and classroom videos of implementation are available online, free of charge.[3])

Student Impacts

A majority of the teachers in the San Diego experiment attributed the enhanced English language development to students "physicalizing" the language, in accordance with the conceptual framework put forward by Mages (2006). The teachers said that movement and gesture helped ELLs learn and remember vocabulary words. "It's the kinesthetic piece," one teacher recalled. "ELL students are *hearing* it. They're *doing* it. They are *understanding* it. It's huge."

The teacher added, "It's hearing it and doing it *themselves*. This is how people learn. It's different from sitting at the table."

This observation supports Mages's argument that students' simultaneous use of their bodies and voices boosts their comprehension and

---

3. Video: http://sites.uci.edu/class/first-grade/theater-first-grade/grade-1-theater-lesson-1/

memory. Arts-based lessons provide visual, auditory, and kinesthetic inputs that, when combined, powerfully signal to students the importance of the new information so that they will integrate it with existing knowledge. Such learning helps students organize, rehearse, and recall material encountered in other lessons (that remains in working memory) and transfer it into long-term memory. Different types of perception and processing are reinforced and strengthened as they work both separately and in conjunction, enhancing mental activity, and assisting the transfer of information from working to long-term memory (Shams & Seitz, 2008).

A kindergarten teacher spoke fondly of a boy who, for the first month of school, spoke just in Spanish. She talked to him but could not tell if he understood her. A turning point came during a lesson about a grumpy bear. The teacher asked the students to act out the bear's feelings; this helped this boy tremendously. Once he fed the make-believe scenario into his knowledge base and internalized the grumpy bear's mood, he could act out these feelings and associate them with vocabulary words. With each TAP lesson after that, he became more vocal and participatory.

A 1st-grade theater lesson focused on nursery rhymes, highlighting how a teacher might scaffold language learning and comprehension. First, the teaching artist asked students to repeat after him, imitating his sing-song, rhythmic tone. In expressive voices, the students repeated, "Jack-and-Jill-went-up-the-hill-to-fetch-a-pail-of-wa-ter." This emphasis on rhythmic enunciation, coupled with pitch variation, provided students with a syntactic framework for correct pronunciation, understanding, and memorization. Next, they began making movements while repeating the rhyme, physically defining the phrase.

As the lesson continued, the teacher divided the children into groups to act out their own (different) versions of the story (maybe Jack and Jill are not siblings but good friends, or Jack decides he does not want to go up the hill). A year older than the kindergartners were when they enacted the Goldilocks tale, these students could add characters or plot lines and change the story any way they chose. This interpretation exercise, designed with insights from cognitive learning theory, led to stronger, more lasting effects by encouraging creativity and student participation.

Organic environments such as those associated with arts activities engage students and encourage them to draw on existing knowledge, which promotes language development. Such contextual learning is both meaningful and memorable for the student. Children were excited about TAP, as shown by a boost in attendance on lesson days (Brouillette, Childress-Evans, Hinga, & Farkas, 2014). Teacher interview data also indicated that students were spontaneously practicing TAP activities outside of TAP time. This signified a level of student engagement and participation that was pivotal in building an effective learning environment. As one teacher observed: "The primary benefit to the teacher was the engagement of students, obviously. To see that every student has equal access to this curriculum and that they willingly and eagerly participate is huge."

Classroom Culture

Teacher-led classroom instruction limits interaction. Confident talkers answer the questions posed by the teacher, while students who are not comfortable speaking or perhaps do not have the language skills to comprehend and/or respond, remain silent. Such limited interactions can put learners who do not have the tools to participate at a disadvantage. But including arts activities is one way to encourage student participation. A kindergarten teacher commented:

> I think for some of my ELL students, it (TAP) was good for them to be able to show me, instead of having to tell me. I have a couple of them who go to speech and it was good to see them act and they didn't have to explain and feel embarrassed or anything. They were just moving around and doing it that way.

The TAP coordinator noticed that many students who initially were afraid to speak did so when they were provided a line to read. "Feeling confident enough to verbalize something, even if it's given to them, is a good thing," she said. A 1st-grade teacher echoed this sentiment: "The language alone was amazing. Kids who don't ever speak [will] speak. You see a lot of kids shine that you don't expect to shine.... So it was really fun to see some new friends shine. That [elicited] a new sense of confidence."

To become orally proficient, students must feel comfortable in their social environment. The interactive arts activities promoted a supportive and collaborative classroom environment. One teacher said:

> I think of a couple of kids who are really shy when you're just discussing something in class ... they're the ones who are spinning and dancing! So I think it changed a lot of them in that they felt more comfortable around each other. And if you can go do that in front of each other, why can't you work as a group in the class? Because you've already been silly and had fun together. It just made ... our classroom community seem tighter and better.

Another teacher observed, "We have a very overactive group of boys. We really saw them shine in dance ... really take it on and really like it. And it built such a sense of community for our class. Kids that don't like each other were changing partners and dancing."

Teachers also mentioned their use of TAP strategies to mitigate some potential behavior issues that can arise when students are invited to interact in unaccustomed ways. One of the dance lessons utilizes an exercise in which children create a "personal bubble." The teacher asks the students to stretch out their arms and legs and imagine that a bubble surrounds their extended limbs. The children then danced around the classroom, starting slowly then moving quickly. Staffers encouraged the children to move their bodies creatively; the only rule was that they could not break out of their bubble or enter into anyone else's bubble. One kindergarten teacher recalled that she found this exercise particularly beneficial in teaching her class about respecting personal space:

> I have a lot of kids that can't keep their hands to themselves. But when they're in [TAP activities] they're just different kids. . . . When they're moving around the room, they have to keep their personal space. Even when they're moving fast and slow at different speeds, they still watch where they're going and I think they're more conscious of how other people are feeling and moving.

INTEGRATING DRAMA AND DANCE ACTIVITIES

Without question, one of the benefits of the Teaching Artist Project to the San Diego schools was the technical expertise of the trained teaching artists. But a teaching artist is not necessary for the integration of drama and dance into the primary grades. As a teaching artist exclaimed to a group of San Diego teachers, "You're already doing theater. You just don't know it yet!" Because kindergarten and 1st-grade teachers routinely read out loud to their classes, most of these professionals found it easy to guide children in dramatizing short scenes in stories. Teachers who participated in the TAP program reported their comfort in showing children how to identify the beginning, middle, and end of a scene, as well as ways to use facial expressions and gestures to convey feelings.

Some teachers felt less comfortable about teaching dance. But in such cases, after the year of weekly teaching artist visits ended, most schools found the dance lessons valuable enough that they rearranged their schedule, appointing one teacher to teach dance to all classes across the grade level. Another alternative was recruiting parent volunteers. Involving parents with an interest in drama or dance not only helped teachers but also served to engage community members and, in the process, further engage students.

New teachers, who came into schools after the teaching artist year, found the online materials made available to teachers particularly beneficial.[4] An after-school teacher who has implemented TAP lessons on her own (separate from the Teaching Artist Project) suggested, "It helped me to take notes on the videos and use these notes to guide my instruction when necessary." She also noted it was helpful to

> Have a clear idea of the activities so that the flow of the lesson is not disrupted. The teacher may want to write an outline on the board for both students and teacher to refer to throughout the lesson so that the teacher does not need to rely on looking down at her notes. The more familiar and comfortable the teacher is with the plans, the more smoothly the lesson will flow.

She concluded by commenting that "a background in arts is not necessary. These [lesson] plans can be followed like any other [ones] and only require a thorough and clear understanding of the material and the particular set of students the teacher is working with." (The link to the lesson plan is at top of each lesson webpage.)

Keys to Success

Case studies documented the successful implementation of the Teaching Artist Project at two schools with differing demographic profiles that suggested pivotal elements in success. In one school, 77.8% of the students were ELLs (with 87.2% of them identified as Hispanic) and 96% of the students were eligible for the free or reduced-price lunch program. At the other school, 27% of the students were ELLs (with 52.9% identified as Hispanic) and 72% of students were eligible for the free or reduced-price lunch program.

Teacher Collaboration and Ownership. Teachers worked together closely at both sites. After 1 year of co-teaching with a teaching artist, mentor teachers for each grade level facilitated meetings with their colleagues to generate ideas and swap strategies. Teachers became resources for one another, collaborating on lesson planning and sharing what worked and what did not work from previous weeks. Cooperation fostered creativity and prompted teachers to be resourceful in finding ways to integrate TAP strategies throughout the curriculum. As one kindergarten teacher recalled, "We would talk about the different projects and all see how we could take those art projects and activities and incorporate it in the curriculum because we didn't want it to be separated from the academics." Another teacher allowed that hearing colleagues reveal their initial nervousness or awkwardness helped build her confidence.

4. Video: https://sites.uci.edu/class/kindergarten/dance/grade-k-dance-lesson-1/

Fidelity in Implementation. The success of academic programs is strongly linked to fidelity in implementation strategies (O'Donnell, 2008). Teachers at both schools made a commitment to teach all their TAP lessons the year after they had co-taught with the teaching artists. Both schools decided to stick with the same schedule they had adopted for the teaching artists, with arts lessons provided at the same time of day, on the same day of the week. Teachers jokingly pointed out that students would remember the time for the TAP lesson, even if a teacher forgot: "We go through all the lessons because we have that special time and that's the time we do it. And the kids wouldn't let us forget!"

A 2nd-grade mentor teacher in one of the schools explained that a temporary classroom hosted the arts lessons; thus, the teachers had to arrange their schedules to allow for TAP lessons: "We picked the time the same day so that we followed one another. . . . I was first, and then I wrote all the stuff on the board for what the lesson was about. And then the next teacher came in and could use that for their lesson. And then the last teacher could come in and use it."

Curriculum Integration. Researchers have found that curriculum integration, an interdisciplinary approach to core skills and concepts, is an effective teaching and learning method (Beane, 1997). Resource teachers designed TAP lessons to include, not only an arts component, but an application to literacy as well. At both the studied schools, teachers frequently incorporated TAP concepts and tools throughout the curriculum. Teachers used pantomime techniques for vocabulary study, dance for math (counting beats), improvisation techniques for reading aloud, and warm-up routines to win students' attention and/or restore classroom order.

Such an integrative approach is well aligned with the objectives of the Common Core standards. Drawing upon arts lessons is one way to reinforce core concepts such as collaborative conversations and clear expression. One kindergarten teacher noted:

> After we did our voice projection when the kids were speaking during "Think Aloud," we would use classroom voices. And then we would use our quiet voices in the library, you know, our low voices, and our gruff voices when we're acting out characters, but never when we're talking to the teacher or our peer students.

Improvising Scenes

Children can tap into their own personal experiences when they improvise scenes or simulate actions through dramatizations and creative movement. By using their voices to dramatize the characters' words and their bodies to recreate the characters' actions—students learn to connect the decontextualized text used in the classroom to their experiences outside of school. Through engaging their imagination in this way, children increase their ability to comprehend and mentally simulate the events, characters, and concepts described.

Even if they do not initially comprehend all of the words, English learners can understand the plot and feelings of the characters in a story through dramatization. By imaginatively touching, seeing, and experiencing the significance of the words in the text, children inject themselves into the situation described by the author and grasp the meaning of events in human terms. This allows each child to go beyond the limitations of his or her English language vocabulary and engage with literature on the child's actual developmental level.

Arts-based learning also introduces the attention-grabbing aspect of novelty. When teachers repeatedly use the same teaching methods, children become habituated to them. Sprinkling creative arts activities into a curriculum that has become routine not only engages young learners but also serves as one way to incorporate standards-based learning and boost academic performance, including the fundamental literacy skills of English language learners.

Building Literacy Skills

Some useful skills, like riding a bicycle, are learned primarily through practice. Learning "sight words," which do not follow the usual rules of phonics, is another example. How can a teacher make this process interesting enough to help students remember the lesson content? Group spelling, a version of tableaux—or the depiction of a scene onstage through the postures assumed by motionless actors—is one strategy. The teacher divides the class into groups of five or six and gives the whole class a word to spell out by physically arranging themselves so that they spell out that word with their bodies. The challenge of doing this suddenly makes that word memorable. More than one word can be introduced, as long as the students stay interested.

A similar approach can be used to clarify the meaning of advanced academic language, such as scientific terms. Teachers can introduce words like *hibernation* or *gravitation* by having students perform a humorous micro-skit. Groups of students are invited to mime the process of a bear going to sleep for the winter or a shopper with too many packages losing his or her balance. Alternatively, a word like *metamorphosis* could be depicted by sketching a caterpillar, a cocoon, and a butterfly. Reminders could be given later in the week, with the introduction "Remember when we . . ."

Possibilities to Consider

- Would you like to be able to work daily oral language practice into your classroom schedule?
- Are there times when children become so restless that acting out a brief scene from a story might provide them a welcome chance to move around and to physicalize the actions they have been reading about and practice speaking?
- Might drama and creative movement activities enrich your morning literacy block?

VISUAL THINKING STRATEGIES

Both the 2009 reading framework of the National Assessment of Educational Progress (NAEP) and the Common Core State Standards require students to read a high and increasing proportion of informational text as they advance through the grades. Visual images can be used in varied ways to help K–5 teachers teach advanced reading skills. The basic technique—created in the late 1980s by Abigail Housen, a cognitive psychologist in the Harvard Graduate School of Education, and veteran museum educator Philip Yenawine—was developed as an elementary school curriculum. Their Visual Thinking Strategies (Yenawine, 2013) technique uses details of artworks to enhance students' understanding and nurture verbal language skills. Robertson (2006) described the Visual Thinking Strategies (VTS) method as follows:

1. The teacher selects an interesting picture or painting.
2. A copy of this picture is placed on an overhead projector.
3. Students are asked, "Please look at the picture silently for a minute and think about what you see. What's going on in the picture?"
4. After a minute, the teacher opens up the question to the room: "What do you see in the picture?"
5. When a student offers a qualitative statement, the teacher asks for more information: "You said the picture looks old. What makes you say that?"
6. Next the teacher asks, "What more can we find?" Students share their observations and provide justification. The teacher summarizes, without inserting information.
7. The discussion goes on until students have shared all they can about the picture.
8. The teacher summarizes what the students have said, focusing on critical thinking.

9. For older students, the teacher may follow up by either having the students write a few sentences about what they have discovered or read a text related to the picture.

Because the works of art are open to a multiplicity of interpretations, VTS provides educators with an opportunity to prepare students for a world where critical thinking and communication skills are essential keys to professional success. Teachers act as facilitators, paraphrasing each student's comments and showing a link between different observations when appropriate. Students learn to support their opinions with evidence, listen respectfully to others, share information and ideas, and construct meaning with their peers. After completing the 10-week VTS curriculum, teachers reported that the majority of students learned to read more quickly, possessed greater comprehension skills, and became more capable of expressing entire concepts and completing whole thoughts in a sentence (Longhenry, 2005).

Making Thinking Visible

Researchers at Harvard's Project Zero have developed strategies, called Visible Thinking, that extend the development of students' thinking skills across the curriculum. Through including thinking dispositions, Visible Thinking not only addresses students' ability to use their thinking skills with prompting from a teacher, but also strengthens curiosity, alertness to opportunities to make use of their thinking skills, and the inclination to take advantage of such opportunities. The goal is two-fold: (1) to cultivate students' thinking skills and dispositions and (2) to deepen content area learning. Ideally, these short, easy-to-learn mini strategies will extend and deepen students' thinking and become part of the fabric of everyday classroom life. The easiest way to get started with Visible Thinking—the use of thinking routines—has much in common with Visual Thinking Strategies.

One Visible Thinking routine, "What Makes You Say That?" is essentially a broader application of the VTS questions, which ask students to interpret what they see and then point to the evidence on which their interpretation is based. Other routines, such as "Think Puzzle Explore," "Think Pair Share," and "I used to think . . . Now I think . . ." focus on related thinking skills, such as setting the stage for deeper inquiry, active reasoning and explanation, or reflecting on how/why one's thinking has changed. These options enable teachers to deepen student thinking across the curriculum. Repeatedly using one routine—for example, "What Makes You Say That?"—helps students become accustomed to going beyond fleeting impressions and taking a closer look at the evidence that supports their inferences.

The Impact of Shared Experience

The impact of such experience with collaborative inquiry goes beyond academics. As children develop, their interactions with teachers and caregivers influence how they become aware of their own internal worlds (Siegel, 2012). When a teacher introduces an interesting picture and draws a group of children into an engaging discussion, sharing their interest and excitement, this experience builds a sense of community. Each child feels seen and heard. Learning becomes fun. Lev Vygotsky (1986) observed that the shared experiences of interpersonal relationships provide a rich source for people's mental lives, supporting the development of their thought processes and internal states.

Elliot Eisner (2002) pointed out that "culture" carries two meanings. In the anthropological sense, a culture is a shared way of life. In the biological sense, a culture is a medium for growing things. Both definitions have importance for educators: Schools provide the conditions for a shared way of life yet also serve as a culture for growing things. What schools grow—or at least aspire to—are minds. They do this by creating a designed environment that shapes the ideas, values, and skills that become a significant part of children's cognitive repertoire. Arts integration enriches the range of experiences that these developing minds are invited to explore.

Lesson plans, videos, and resources mentioned in this and other chapters may be accessed at: http://sites.uci.edu/educ104donline/

CHAPTER 3

Making Meaning of Narrative Text

Even in the caves the human habitations were adorned with the colored pictures that kept alive to the senses experiences with the animals that were so closely bound with the lives of the humans. (John Dewey, 1934)

Long before humans began to build towns and cities, the arts played an important role in connecting people within a community. The prior chapter considers how the arts support the development of oral language skills. This chapter focuses on dramatic narrative, which tells the stories of people's lives. It pays special attention to how arts-based strategies can help students make meaning through reading and discussion, thus adding an affective dimension to Eisner's (2002) description of the arts' role in building cognitive understanding. Quoting the words of Leo Tolstoy (1897/1994)—author of *War and Peace* and *Anna Karenina*—art has the capacity to do all these things:

> [E]voke reverence for each man's dignity, for every animal's life, it can evoke the shame of luxury, of violence, of revenge, of using for one's pleasure objects that are a necessity for other people.

Tolstoy contended that great art has a contagious quality that is accessible to every person. The power of a work of art can be found in how it unites people in the same feeling. He argued passionately that even traditional stories and folk songs have the potential to build a sense of the shared humanity of people from different backgrounds. Yet, in an era of high-stakes testing, the English language arts curriculum can become so focused on mastering grade-level vocabulary and the mechanics of reading that these grander themes can be crowded out. To broaden our perspective, we will take a brief look at the power of written narrative from a historical viewpoint, focusing on the impact of the invention of the Greek alphabet in about 800 B.C.E.

HOW WRITTEN NARRATIVE INFLUENCES THINKING

Before the invention of writing, humans had to rely on memory, drawings, and musical chants to preserve important information (Egan, 1997). The problem was that memory can be inaccurate and drawings and chants can be open to varied interpretations. So when communities introduced the written word, it was revolutionary. Writing things down extended the natural limits of human memory. A portion of the writer's memories could be preserved on clay tablets, papyrus, or parchment. Once it became possible for human memory to be externalized using written language, the writer's attentional system was freed up to focus on other pressing needs.

Kieran Egan (1997) reminds us that a number of scholars have credited the "Greek miracle" of the 5th century B.C.E.—which gave birth to democracy, logic, philosophy, history, drama, and so on—to the development and spread of alphabetic literacy. In oral cultures, knowledge must be continually repeated so people do not forget and lose it. Once writing became available, it was possible to take a more detached attitude toward memory and accumulate far more facts. Literacy could provide access to a treasure house of stored data and ideas. Writing also made it possible for individuals to access the stories told by people they had never met. For example, *The Histories* of Herodotus had a dramatic impact in ancient Greece, making the reader (or listener, if it were read aloud) a kind of witness, vicariously present at the events described.

The vicarious experience provided in written narratives greatly expanded the knowledge base that readers could call upon when solving problems (Egan, 1997). Ideas could be shared with people they had never met. In a sense, a child who is learning to read is recapitulating one of the most exciting discoveries in human history. Ever since ancient times, the written word has evoked a sense of magic and mystery. This is worth keeping in mind in an era when children accustomed to watching television may feel they are learning to read only because adults say they *must*. Such young readers may never discover the joys of reading for pleasure.

According to the American Time Use Survey (2017) published by the U.S. Bureau of Labor Statistics, from 2004 to 2017 the number of Americans who read for pleasure on a given day fell by more than 30%. This is somewhat understandable. Unlike the genetically encoded skills of walking and talking, learning to read requires considerable conscious effort. The challenge is to make sure that the effort involved brings with it a sense of discovery, an "aha!" feeling that turns reading for pleasure into an exhilarating adventure. This sense of excitement is not derived from mastering the mechanics of reading or memorizing vocabulary words. Students must be able read and discuss narratives that provide meaningful insights into the culture around them.

Stories Support Social and Cognitive Development

> We do not regard aesthetic education as in any sense a fringe under-taking, a species of "frill." We see it as integral to the development of persons—to their cognitive, perceptual, emotional, and imaginative development. We see it as part of the human effort (so often forgotten today) to seek a greater coherence in the world. (Greene, 2001, p. 7)

In the spring of 1994, kindergarten teacher and MacArthur Fellow Vivian Paley gave a lecture at Rice University titled "Abraham Lincoln and My Mother Were Not At Risk" (Brouillette, 1997). She pointed out that with public schools focusing on an increasingly narrow spectrum of measurable skills, they had been ignoring important human variables, including the ones that most children would consider central to describing who they are. Noting that by current standards Abraham Lincoln and her own mother would have been considered "at risk," Paley said that such a label can blind educators to the social–emotional needs of these children.

Paley argued that for children categorized as "at risk" to build the strength of character needed to lead a fulfilling life, they must be aided in gathering the range of personal resources that nourish a strong and resilient individual identity. To do this, they must learn to see themselves, not as bundles of deficits, but as individuals with stories that are integral to a human whole. Until this century, the vast majority of children learned about the world beyond their personal experience not by going to school but by listening to the stories of family, friends, and acquaintances. Over time, these stories coalesced to form the cultural backdrop against which their personal narrative, the story of their own lives, unfolded. Alasdair MacIntyre (1981) observed:

> Deprive children of stories and you leave them unscripted, anxious stutterers in their actions as in their words. Hence there is no way to give us an understanding of any society, including our own, except through the stock of stories which constitute its initial dramatic resources. (p. 216)

Children continually share and retell stories with their peers—as do adults. This informal retelling of tales has more than a trivial importance. As James Q. Wilson (1994) wrote, Greek literature began with the telling and retelling of the story of Ulysses. The biblical stories of the friendship of Ruth and Naomi, the battle of David and Goliath, and the travails of Job were spoken long before they were written. Humans need to explain, justify, and instruct. It is impossible to conceive of a society that does not have and preserve a legacy of stories.

Building on a similar insight, Vivian Paley (Brouillette, 1997) suggested that children who are nourished by enough good stories would, in due time, be able to learn everything else they needed to know. Drawing on her own experience, she suggested that, in sharing their stories, children become part of a coherent classroom culture where each student's story is known and forms part of a larger whole. When children tell or write their stories, they not only practice basic literacy skills (with an enthusiasm not always shown at other times of the school day), but they also create a new kind of window out of the classroom. Through this window, children, who migrate among the separate, disconnected worlds of home, school, and television episodes, received opportunities to contemplate the meaning of their experiences. How can teachers help children make sense of all the stories they bring with them to school or encounter in class?

Expanding Comprehension Skills

In kindergarten, children are already learning to identify characters, settings, and important events in a story. By 2nd grade, students are learning to compare and contrast the characters, settings, and plots presented by different authors. Traditionally, the skill of comparing and contrasting is taught in a manner that is strongly language based. This means that students must (1) understand the words the teacher uses to explain the assignment and (2) have a command of the vocabulary needed to describe the similarities and differences they perceive. In a class with English learners or individuals with a wide range of oral language skills, not all students might have the vocabulary to understand what the teacher is asking and give an appropriate response without visual aids.

Using visual images to reinforce verbal explanations will make compare/contrast lessons more accessible to diverse learners. In the early grades, comparing and contrasting often involves exploring fundamental binary oppositions (shy/outgoing, old/young). Portraying binary opposites through pictures (entrance/exit, up/down, ocean/land) can be an effective strategy. Instead of merely focusing on individual words, children learn to build concepts by investigating pairs of opposites (or antonyms) like day/night. Bringing up examples of binary opposites when the teacher is reading a story aloud also encourages children to think more deeply about what they have heard.

When reading a picture book such as Jane Yolen's *Owl Moon*, a teacher might point to a picture and ask: "Why are these people wearing warm clothing?" Such a question not only causes children to think more deeply about the story and the significance of its setting, but may also lead to further questions. What is the opposite of *warm*? Why are the people walking at night? What is the opposite of *night*? Through such simple questioning techniques, the teacher amplifies students' understanding by encouraging them to think about how the story's setting and context shaped events in the story. The discussion of antonyms also doubles the potential vocabulary learned by children participating in the discussion.

In her kindergarten classroom, Vivian Paley encouraged students' creativity through a "storytelling curriculum" that consisted of two activities: dictation and dramatization. First, a child dictates her or his story to the teacher. Then the class dramatizes the story. Patricia M. Cooper (2005) described the process this way: As the child dictates, the teacher acts as scribe, editor, and initial audience. Ideally, this occurs during center or choice time. A typical opening exchange might be: "How does your story begin?" "One day . . ." The teacher might ask for clarification about a confusing point ("I don't understand. How many babies were there?"). Or the teacher might pause writing to simply appreciate the story: "Wow! What an amazing day you had. . . ."

For the sake of efficiency, these stories can be limited to one page. The teacher rereads what the child dictated to offer an opportunity for revision. Then the author chooses classmates to act out the various characters from the list of children waiting for a turn to play a role in dramatizing a story. Classmates who are not actors will make up the audience. To hold the children's interest, the dramatization typically occurs on the same day that the story is told. Usually, teachers use the dramatization as a transition activity—for example, after center time and before lunch.

When the dramatization takes place, the teacher first reads the story to the class to alert the actors and audience to the plot. Then they read it aloud again as the actors step into their roles. The teacher serves as director and producer, offering suggestions to help foster dramatic interpretation, such as: "How can you show the class that the monster surprised you?" However, expectations for actors' dramatic performance are relatively low. Except on special occasions, each dramatization is a one-time-through, no-rehearsal event. Also, a "no touching" rule is a good idea during the dramatization, so as to avoid accidents when the plot line involves karate kicks, putting robbers in jail, or even placing babies in cribs.

Over time children have the opportunity to expand their storytelling and acting abilities, aided by feedback from the audience. They gain a better grasp of where stories come from and acquire skills in sequencing, plot development, characterization, and using imagination. The dictation session gives the teacher a chance to engage in an open-ended conversation with each of the children, helping to expand their vocabulary, sentence length, and verbal expression.

DEEPENING CHILDREN'S UNDERSTANDING OF NARRATIVE

As children's narrative skills develop, they are able to deal with longer plot sequences. Many stories favored by children in the primary grades bear a structure similar to traditional myths, with the action unfolding as the destined outgrowth of the character of the hero or heroine, king or queen, sage, or villain. The resilience and optimism of these heroic tales have much to recommend them. Contemporary authors continue to use archetypes from myths and traditions in their narratives.

Let's look at the Disney version of Cinderella as an example. The heroine is an orphan who is mistreated by her mean-spirited stepmother and stepsisters. Yet, she remains kind and patient, showing great stoicism in coping with her daily chores and impoverishment. Eventually, she is saved by her fairy godmother, who enables her to go to the royal ball, where her beauty and noble nature awaken the prince's interest. But the evil stepmother and her daughters see people around them as mere stepping-stones to use for realizing their desires; they do everything they can to keep Cinderella "in her place" (working for them). Still, despite the obstacles the evil stepmother puts in the way of the new romance, the prince still recognizes Cinderella's inner beauty, even when it is disguised by ragged clothes and poor surroundings.

Cinderella is virtuous and courageous, as are other Disney princesses. Yet, there are limitations associated with these archetypal stories. Each person in the story has an in-born character that determines their actions Although childhood is a stage of life defined by development, these stories portray character as a static trait, like a snapshot frozen in time. Such simplicity makes the story accessible to young children. But if more complex stories are not offered in the intermediate grades, children can receive the impression that individuals are born either good or bad. Fortunately, students in grades 3 through 5 naturally develop an interest in more detailed explanations.

> If you tell a typical five-year-old the story of Cinderella, you are not likely to be asked "What means of locomotion does the Fairy Godmother use?" nor to be quizzed about where she is and what she does when she isn't active in the story. But if you tell a typical ten-year-old the equally fantastic story of Superman, you will need to explain his supernatural powers by reference to his birth on the planet Krypton and to the different molecular structure of our sun from that of his home star and so on. (Egan, 1997, p. 71)

Harry Potter: A Male Cinderella

Although the popularity of Harry Potter books by J.K. Rowling has faded somewhat since they were first published, they remain an excellent after-lunch read-aloud choice for students in the intermediate grades. At this age, students are becoming aware of their own capacity for growth and change, as well as the fluidity of the cultural environment in which they are immersed. The way the Harry Potter stories combine fairytale structure with character development provides plenty of room for discussion of how the characters' choices drive the plot. Each book traces the events of one school year. When readers first meet Harry, he is a scrawny, miserable, black-haired boy with glasses. With his hand-me-down clothes and spectacles held together by tape, Harry Potter appears to be a classic "loser," a boy everyone makes fun of and takes advantage of. Yet, it is Harry with whom readers identify.

When Harry Potter gets to Hogwarts in the first book, teachers may wish to introduce a comparison/contrast lesson to alert students to similarities between Harry Potter and Cinderella (King, 2000). After reviewing the story of Cinderella, students can brainstorm ways that Harry's story is similar to—or different from—that of Cinderella. As the teacher jots their ideas on the board, students might experience an "aha!" moment as they begin to see Harry Potter from a different perspective. As an orphan, Harry has been grudgingly raised by the Dursleys, his only living relatives. His aunt Petunia and uncle Vernon spoil their son, Dudley, while treating Harry like a servant. Just as Cinderella was expected to cater to her stepmother and stepsisters, Harry is expected to do all the household chores. A fairy godmother assists Cinderella. Harry is rescued by Hagrid, a half-giant with magical powers and a pink umbrella.

The rescue does not, however, instantly heal Harry's greatest affliction, the feeling of being unloved and unwanted. As Mother Teresa observed, "The most terrible poverty is loneliness, and the feeling of being unloved" (Mah, 1999, p. xii). Such treatment by caregivers can undermine a child's sense of self-worth. Beneath the fairytale trappings, the real gift Hagrid brings Harry is a renewed sense of self-esteem. After years of mistreatment, Harry (like Cinderella) had tacitly accepted his fate. Then, through an unexpected turn of events, he is transported to a school where people recognize his true worth. It takes Harry a while to feel like he really belongs at Hogwarts. Over time, though, Harry and his friends Ron and Hermione come to feel at home and find great meaning in their experiences at Hogwarts.

Storyboarding. Chapter 1 examines the function of art in terms of formulating representations of experience (Eisner, 2002). For children, as for adults, the results of thinking are evanescent unless stabilized by inscribing them in a lasting material. Yet, when students listen to a story or read aloud in a group, they may become so focused on what characters are doing at the moment that they lose comprehension of the overall plot. Teachers can provide an alternate way for students to comprehend a complex narrative by having them re-create a story or chapter's plot, using storyboards to summarize events. Later, as students progress further through a book, they can refer back to the storyboards if they are uncertain about earlier events. Also, students may compare their initial storyboards to see who recognized the details that later proved key.

Essley, Rief, and Rocci (2008) argued that pictures combined with text offer a rich synthesis of information that can both entertain and inform. They demonstrated how low-tech storyboards—using simple stick figures and spare text (just a few key words)—can show students in the intermediate grades a clear path to understanding narrative. Stick figures are easy for children to make. The storyboard can be as short as two squares or as long as a graphic novel. The logical sequencing power of storyboards, combined with the hands-on satisfaction of drawing, allows slower writers and English learners to participate freely.

The storyboard technique can help students in grades 3 through 5 to describe the beginning, middle, and end of a chapter they just heard read aloud, as well as aid in identifying its main events. Working in pairs, students verbally discuss the first and last events of the story, then identify the key events that led to the conclusion. After finishing this exercise, students fill in their storyboards, using images and text. Later on, students can refer to their storyboards to jog their memories during discussions about how an action may have influenced subsequent events—or to arrive at a theory about what might happen next.

Looking Beneath the Surface. Harry Potter is by no means a perfect hero. An average student, he procrastinates when it comes to doing his homework. He is not always on time to class and sometimes trips up when trying to fib his way out of trouble (Knapp, 2003). Once 4th- and 5th-graders become adept at using storyboards, they can look more closely at the impact of characters' choices. What if Harry, Hermione, or Ron had selected a different option in a key situation? By creating an alternative ending for a chapter, based on what happened when Harry or another character made a different choice, students become more aware of how such choices drive the plot. This activity can stimulate thought-provoking class discussions. Questions that teachers reading the first Harry Potter book aloud might choose to explore include:

- How might Harry's experience living with the Dursleys have influenced his attitude toward bullies—for example, when he retrieves Neville's Remembrall after Malfoy grabs it?
- What choices helped the bookish Hermione become a formidable master of spells?

- How do members of the financially struggling Weasley family play a critical role in helping Harry feel at home in the wizarding community and deal with the challenges he encounters?

The Role of Magic. Some students might have questions about the references to witchcraft and wizardry in the Potter books. Popular culture teems with tales of villains who engage in malicious magical practices. On the other hand, history shows numerous cases of traditional healers and early scientists being attacked by superstitious community members who misunderstood their methods. As science fiction writer Arthur C. Clarke (1973) once noted, "Any sufficiently advanced technology is indistinguishable from magic." Like the technology of our own world, the magic in Harry Potter's world is treated as a tool that can be used for either good or evil, depending on the goals of the people using it (Denton, 2002).

In class discussions, teachers can point out that, despite the sprinkling of magic spells, potions, and "witchy" black hats in the Harry Potter series, the books contain no demons. On a metaphoric level, it is the raging emotions that students in the intermediate grades and in middle school must learn to cope with that are personified as fire-breathing dragons (anger, jealousy), dementors (depression, fear), werewolves (severe mood swings), and other monsters. Such distancing techniques can make fierce emotions less daunting to talk about. There are also decided limits to what members of Harry Potter's wizarding world can do, even through magic (Knapp, 2003). As Headmaster Dumbledore himself affirmed: "No spell can reawaken the dead" (Rowling, 2000, p. 697).

What the magical elements do provide is a fresh perspective. In an era when preparation for standardized tests is a major concern, the K–5 curriculum has increasingly been reduced to a predictable routine, with little connection to the fears, hopes, and passions of the very students reading the textbooks. If children find schoolwork dull, lifeless, and unengaging, their curiosity and motivation to learn diminishes. Although fantasy fiction may not suit the tastes of all adults, the genre can feed young students' imaginations and bring classroom discussion to life. Through such conversations, teachers assist students in developing not just a better understanding of a narrative but also a sense of the complexity of human motivations.

As students progress through the Harry Potter series, they can see that even the wise headmaster Dumbledore has made mistakes and lives with searing regrets. Professor Snape, whom Harry has long distrusted, turns out to have had a tragic history—and been the bravest of friends. The presentation of human fallibility and contradictions gives the Harry Potter books an unusual depth and complexity for juvenile fiction.

But bad things do happen to good people in the books. Harry's god-father Sirius and fellow student Cedric Diggory are killed. Should young readers be confronted with tragic events? Denton (2002) argued yes:

> I think it is a wiser course of action to let children see something of the world as it is, something of what evil lurks in the hearts of other people, to help them learn the nature of the choices they will have to make, in order that they have a better chance of fending for themselves when there is no longer an adult around to protect them. (p. 30)

Even so, the magical elements of the Harry Potter books make it possible to skip over many real-life complications that might otherwise bog down the plot. The early books in the series portray only Harry, Ron, and Hermione as changing and developing. The other characters seem to be fairytale archetypes, reacting in predictable ways.

Yet, it is possible for a book to use the Cinderella archetype as a metaphor, without depending on a fairy godmother to drive the plot. The next section explores an autobiographic work that takes a real-world—but hopeful—look at the struggles of an unwanted child.

Possibilities to Consider

- Are there times when students become so focused on what characters in a story are doing that their comprehension of the overall plot is lost?
- Might storyboards, using simple stick figures combined with spare text, be useful in jogging students' memories during class discussions?
- Could the storyboards help students describe the beginning, middle, and end of a chapter that has just been read—or to identify the chapter's main events?

Using the Cinderella Archetype as a Literary Lens

In the Harry Potter books, people of various races and ethnicities are depicted within the wizarding world, but the impact of cultural and gender differences is not explored in depth. This section investigates a real-life Cinderella story that addresses human diversity while also looking at the developmental process of an unwanted child who gains the strength, skill, and confidence to overcome abusive circumstances without magic. Egan (1997) argued that, as students near the age for attending middle school, their interest moves from tales about giants to evidence of how tall the tallest person in the world really is. There is a recognition of the stubborn nature of facts and the need for mental constructs that represent this reality. But students at this age lack sufficient real-world knowledge to construct a completely scientific worldview. Literary archetypes can therefore still provide a lens for grasping meaning.

By 5th grade, students already comprehend the basic plots of classic fairytales, myths, folktales, legends, and fables from around the world. Therefore, they can explore stories that broaden their horizons. *Chinese Cinderella: The True Story of an Unwanted Daughter,* the autobiography of physician Adeline Yen Mah (1999), is an inspiring tale of perseverance and hope. Born in Tianjin, China, in 1937, Adeline was considered bad luck by her affluent family because her mother died soon after her birth. When Adeline was a year old, her father married a 17-year-old girl of mixed Chinese and French descent. In Adeline's account, she is called Niang, a Mandarin Chinese term for "mother."

Much of the story takes place during World War II and the Chinese Civil War. After the Japanese army invades China, Adeline and her family flee their hometown and move to the sprawling city of Shanghai. In this cosmopolitan setting, the stepmother Niang becomes the dominant force in the home, giving her five stepchildren English names. However, she either treats the stepchildren—especially Adeline—with cruelty or neglects them. On Adeline's first day in 1st grade, no one picks her up after school, even though she is new to Shanghai and her school is a mile and a half walk from home, through crowded streets. As happens repeatedly in the book, Adeline escapes disaster through her intelligence and the kindness of others. Sprinkled throughout the narrative are numerous parallels between Adeline and Cinderella, which students will find interesting to explore.

In addition, students may find it interesting to learn about an ancient Chinese version of Cinderella. Her name was Yeh-Xian and her story is told as a postscript to Adeline Yen Mah's (1999) book. Tuan Cheng-Shih wrote the tale of Yeh-Xian almost 1,000 years before the first European versions of Cinderella appeared in Giambattista Basile's *Pentamerone* in 1634 Italy and Charles Perrault's *Histoires ou Contes du Temps Passé* in 1697 France. Taking a few moments to compare and contrast Adeline and Yeh-Xian's stories may inspire students to think about Adeline differently. An orphan living with her cruel stepmother, Yeh-Xian is a talented potter who, through her talent and effort, buys an elegant pair of shoes which start a series of events that result in her marrying a local warlord. Like Yeh-Xian, Adeline lacks a fairy godmother. Yet, through her perseverance, she eventually achieves her goal of attending a university in England.

Tracing Subplots. Because Chinese script evolved out of pictures, storyboarding with illustrations is an apt choice for tracing the complex plot of *Chinese Cinderella*. Each chapter could be treated as a separate episode.

Because Adeline's story includes many subplots, storyboarding can help students track the separate dramas of Aunt Baba (who takes care of Adeline as a child until they are forcibly separated), Big Sister (who is pushed into an arranged marriage with a man almost twice her age), and Grandmother Nai Nai (who walks slowly because her feet were bound when she was young). Storyboarding can aid students with comparing and contrasting different parts of the narrative—for example, how Adeline and her siblings are treated when the family lived in Tianjin compared to the way they are dealt with after they move to Shanghai.

Using storyboards to sketch out the contrast between Adeline's painful life at home and popularity at school (before her boarding school days) will enable students to explore the contrast between her two worlds in a concrete way. Three squares at the top of a page could be used to depict events in Adeline's home life, with the bottom three squares reserved for documenting interactions between Adeline and her school friend Wu Chun-mei, who comes from a warm and loving family.

Literature as a Refuge. In *Chinese Cinderella*, the themes of isolation and yearning for acceptance transcend cultures. Adeline ends up learning much from the story (in a book) of the perseverance of another lonely girl even though the two come from entirely different cultures. Adeline's deep reading experience makes all the difference. Teachers can focus attention on this part of the narrative, which describes the benefits of close reading: Adeline borrows a copy of the novel *A Little Princess* (Burnett, 1905) from her school friend Wu Chun-mei, immersing herself in the story of Sara Crewe, a 7-year-old, motherless English girl. Sara started life as an heiress but, after the death of her father, she is penniless and forced to work as a servant girl. Adeline is mesmerized by the tale and later recalls, "I read it again and again, suffered Sara's humiliation, cried over her despair, mourned the loss of her father and savored her final triumph" (Mah, 1999, p. 60).

That Sara eventually changes her life, as a result of her own efforts, grips Adeline's imagination. After reading the novel again and again, she laboriously copies the book before returning it. At night, Adeline sleeps with her copy of the book under her pillow. She recalls:

> For the first time, I realized that adults could be wrong in their judgment about a child. If I tried hard enough to become a princess inside, like Sara Crewe, perhaps I too might someday reverse everyone's poor opinion of me. (Mah, 1999, p. 60)

Holding onto the story of Sara Crewe as if it were a life raft, Adeline doggedly continues her pursuit of academic success, refusing to give in to despair. As she said later:

I read because I have to. It drives everything else from my mind. It lets me escape to find other worlds. The people in my books become more real than anyone else. (Mah, 1999, p. 160)

Living in an era when the option of watching television or a movie is so readily available, students may find it difficult to understand Adeline's passion for books. But the action in a movie shown at a theater flows by so fast that children might not catch all the subtleties in the plot. The option of stopping to reflect (as a reader might on a line of text, savoring every word) is unavailable. There is a special connection with a story when a reader creates his or her own mental images of characters and settings. How might teachers support their students in considering more closely how a story unfolds?

Recognizing the Consequences of Earlier Events. Storyboarding encourages students to slow down and reflect on critical scenes, as well as to focus on how characters' decisions drive the plot. Therefore, storyboarding can be an effective strategy to use in response to specific 5th-grade Common Core standards; for example, ELA-Literacy.RL.5.1 mandates that students should "[q]uote accurately from a text when explaining what the text says explicitly and when drawing inferences from the text."

The *Chinese Cinderella* narrative is rich in pivot points to track. Only two members of Adeline's family consistently show affection for her: Aunt Baba and Grandfather YeYe. However, both lack a voice in the family's affairs because they become financially dependent upon Adeline's father after the family moves to Shanghai. Their transition to dependency is shown in a key scene. YeYe suggests at dinner that the children be given allowances to cover their tram fare to and from school. During his first 2 months in Shanghai, YeYe had provided the children with tram fare, but he has run out of money. Now, his suggestion that the children be given an allowance is bluntly rejected. YeYe's son, Adeline's father, announces that the children have been provided with all that they need. No additional money will be provided to them, except at the discretion of Adeline's father and Niang. Shocked by this, Adeline thinks to herself:

Where is YeYe's own money? Is he no longer head of our family? Why is he suddenly and mysteriously dependent on Father and Niang for pocket money? (Mah, 1999, p. 37)

Students' exploration of the text may take the form of a six-panel storyboard, with the top three panels representing the life Adeline and her siblings had with YeYe in Tianjin, where their grandfather employed seven maids, a cook, a chauffeur, and a rickshaw puller before friction with the

Japanese invaders forced the family to move to Shanghai. Back in Tianjin, the children could invite friends home to play, go for drives on Sundays, and accompany YeYe to lunch at foreign restaurants to sample the cuisine. On the three panels below, the class can add details to the storyboard portraying their very different situation in Shanghai, where they never go out to eat, lack transportation, and are not allowed either to invite friends home or go to friends' houses. What inferences might be drawn about the attitude of their stepmother, Niang, toward Adeline and her siblings?

The next Common Core standard (ELA Literacy.RL.5.2) states, "Determine a theme of a story, drama, or poem from details in the text, including how characters in a story or drama respond to challenges or how the speaker in a poem reflects upon a topic; summarize the text." Chapter 17 offers charged family interactions, ripe for exploration of the characters' motives. YeYe's status within his family suffers again, several years after the Shanghai move, when the family relocates to Hong Kong. One morning, Adeline sees Grandfather Ye Ye going to the living room at 8 o'clock in morning to read the newspapers before breakfast. Adeline spots a pile of thick encyclopedias propped precariously against the ledge above the living room door: They are almost lying in wait, like Niang's son (Fourth Brother, who is furtively lurking nearby), to fall on YeYe's head. Adeline quickly pushes the door open. The heavy books fall to the floor, missing YeYe. Fourth Brother screams in anger. Their father comes out of his bedroom. What has just happened is clear. Yet, Adeline's father does not punish his son for behavior that could have caused grandfather Ye Ye serious injury.

> "Pick up the books!" Adeline's father commanded finally in a stern voice. "Such a racket! Don't you know your mother is still sleeping? Keep your voices down when you play! . . . "
> And that was all. (Mah, 1999, p. 159)

To promote reflection, students might be assigned a "quick write," asking them to take 3 to 4 minutes to explain what Adeline may be feeling when she describes her grandfather in these words: "A tired old man with no one to turn to, imprisoned by his love for his only son, my father" (Mah, 1999, p. 159). After volunteers read their responses, the class may discuss how the behavior of Adeline's father departs from Chinese cultural norms concerning a son's dutiful conduct toward his parents. How may the financial and other challenges caused by the Japanese invasion of China have had an impact on the perceptions and responses of family members?

The Common Core standard ELA-Literacy.RL.5.3 requires students to "[c]ompare and contrast two or more characters, settings, or events in a story or drama, drawing on specific details in the text (e.g., how characters interact)." The wealth that gives Adeline's father power is an outgrowth of opportunities YeYe made possible. But the son is preoccupied with his own survival. Insight into the attitude of Adeline's father may come from focusing on the behavior of his son with Niang, a boy who has been treated like a prince since birth. Teachers might pose this question to their students: Why would Adeline's half-brother respond to the many privileges he has enjoyed by plotting to hurt YeYe?

Before asking students to respond, the teacher might review Chapter 16, in which Adeline is rescued from a boarding school in war-torn Tianjin by the kindly Reine, Niang's older sister. Teachers may ask students to compare/contrast the way Niang treats Adeline with how Aunt Reine treats her in a scene on the ship while Adeline and Reine's family travel from Tianjin to Hong Kong. Arriving in the stateroom where Aunt Reine and her daughter will sleep, Adeline assumes that the small, low cot in their stateroom is for her. But Aunt Reine insists, "It's share and share alike in our family. Nobody is going to be treated differently. Come, let's draw lots to decide who will sleep on the floor" (Mah, 1999, p. 142). When Reine's daughter picks first and receives the slip marked *cot*, she sleeps on the cot without protest for the rest of their time on the ship.

Drawing on insights from *Chinese Cinderella*'s Chapter 17, this discussion may be extended by contrasting the behavior of Aunt Reine's son toward Adeline with Fourth Brother's behavior toward Adeline and YeYe. When they arrive in Hong Kong, Reine's son protests the way that Adeline is always being left behind by Niang when the family goes on an outing. He insists on skipping a ferry ride and picnic, in order to stay home and keep Adeline company (Mah, 1999). Teachers might point out that Aunt Reine's children have become habituated to a family norm of "share and share alike."

But what family norm might Niang's son have internalized? The discussion of this question may be made easier by focusing on a short episode. Riding in a chauffeured car as Niang takes Adeline to boarding school, Fourth Brother suddenly demands to stop and have afternoon tea at the posh Peninsula Hotel. At the restaurant, they are told there is a half-hour wait for a table. Niang haughtily refuses to wait, demanding to be seated immediately; the head waiter complies. Students can discuss how growing up watching Niang's behavior, of which her treatment of the head waiter is just one example, might have encouraged Fourth Brother's tendency to bully others.

The gentle YeYe, a devout Buddhist, receives outward respect from his son but neither empathy nor concern. YeYe's son and grandson—encouraged by Niang—have become accustomed to pushing others out of the way to get what they want. They have come to approach life as if it were a dogfight, where one is either on the top or on the bottom. But the struggle to stay on top is never-ending. Insecure about his position within the family, Fourth

Brother may have set the booby trap for YeYe to capture his father's attention and perhaps to enjoy the thrill of getting away with forbidden behavior.

King Lear. Because Niang does not wish to have Adeline in the house, Adeline is shuttled off to boarding school, where she is lonely and develops a deep sense of empathy for her grandfather. When her high school class reads Shakespeare's *King Lear* aloud, Adeline bursts out crying. She is struck by how the king's plight mirrors that of YeYe. Having given everything he has to his daughters, Lear finds himself abused by them. As with *A Little Princess*, Adeline has discovered a literary work that epitomizes a painful situation in her family. Feelings she had repressed suddenly overwhelm her. For the second time, we see Adeline achieve a sense of catharsis through reading an English narrative that movingly mirrors a crisis in her life or family. This raises the question of whether there are inherent aspects of human nature that may be reflected in all cultures.

Teachers may choose to pose this question by introducing the idea of archetypes, people (such as heroes or mentors) or phenomena (such as friendship or betrayal) that can be found across cultures. Tragedy embodies a specific type of archetype: human flaws such as arrogance, greed, or manipulation (of other human beings, using them as tools to get what one wants). Such human propensities are what ethical codes around the world were set up to combat. An introductory discussion could be followed by an assignment in which students write a brief persuasive essay, arguing for or against the idea that certain human dilemmas tend to appear repeatedly —across cultures and generations.

Alternatively, teachers may choose to lead a discussion in which students explore similarities between YeYe and King Lear. For example, Lear was not only a father but also a king. In Tianjin, YeYe headed his family and was responsible for its well-being. When King Lear gave away his authority to his unworthy elder daughters, he doomed himself and sent all Britain into chaos. After YeYe failed to foresee and prevent his son's attempt to grab control of the family's finances, the hierarchal sense of order that had served the family well in Tianjin fell apart. YeYe's five older grandchildren—along with his daughter Aunt Baba and YeYe himself—were miserable, Adeline most of all. The tragedy of YeYe, like that of Lear, was that he was an essentially good, but flawed, person whose decisions ultimately led to heartbreak for him and for his family.

CLASSIC STORY STRUCTURES

This chapter looks at multiple versions of the Cinderella story. Reading and discussing stories that focus on archetypal human dilemmas is an effective way to engage students on an emotional level, while reaching out to those who might be dealing with challenges they are hesitant to mention. Influential writers, ranging from Carl Jung to Joseph Campbell, Bruno Bettelheim, and Sir James George Frazer, have commented on common plots found in literary works. Christopher Booker's (2004) book, *The Seven Basic Plots*, offers some interesting ideas in this regard. The plots he describes include the following:

- Rags to Riches: A disadvantaged protagonist acquires power, success, or a mate (*Cinderella, Jane Eyre, Harry Potter, Aladdin, David Copperfield*).
- The Quest: A protagonist and companions set out to acquire an important object or arrive at a location (*The Lord of the Rings, The Odyssey, Watership Down*).
- Voyage and Return: A protagonist travels to a strange land and returns wiser (*Alice in Wonderland, The Hobbit, The Wizard of Oz, The Chronicles of Narnia*).
- Overcoming the Monster: A protagonist sets out to defeat an antagonistic force (*Star Wars, Dune, The Hunger Games, Jaws, The Terminator, James Bond*).
- Comedy: A light and humorous tale in which a conflict becomes more and more confusing, then is resolved in single clarifying event (http://sites.uci.edu/educ104donline/ re's comedies).
- Tragedy: A protagonist's character flaw or error is their undoing, evoking pity upon their fall (*Romeo and Juliet, Julius Caesar, Madame Bovary, Citizen Kane*).
- Rebirth: An event prompts the main character to change their ways and become a better person (*A Christmas Carol, Beauty and the Beast, The Snow Queen*).

Examples of lesson plans, videos, resources, and teaching materials mentioned in this chapter may be accessed at the following website: http://sites.uci.edu/educ104donline/

CHAPTER 4

Making Meaning from Informational Texts

Out of students from 49 nations that participated in the 2011 Progress in International Reading Literacy Study (PIRLS), U.S. 4th-graders ranked second in reading literature and fifth in reading for information; students will need the latter skill daily at the university level and for most future careers (Duchouquette, Loschert, & Barth, 2014). But current trends are not encouraging. On the 2016 PIRLS, the United States ranked 15th among nations on its 4th-graders' overall reading achievement. Peggy G. Carr, acting commissioner of the National Center for Education Statistics, said:

> Our fourth graders declined both in terms of their average score, as well as in their standing relative to other education systems. We see the same trend in the latest PIRLS results that we've been noticing for some time on other international assessments. Countries that were our peers have surpassed us while some that used to do worse than us are now our peers. (National Center for Education Statistics, 2017)

Equally disturbing for U.S. educators is American students' academic progress after 4th grade. The United States placed 24th among 73 countries on the Programme for International Student Assessment's 2015 reading test taken by 15-year-olds (Heim, 2016). In contrast, Canada placed third on the PISA assessment. Educators and policymakers face an interesting question: Why should Canada place so much higher than the United States in reading? Like the United States, Canada is a large, diverse nation with local school boards, no federal control over public schools, and powerful teacher unions. The way reading has been taught in U.S. public schools might have something to do with it.

During the 1990s, literacy research led by Harvard professor Jean Chall gave rise to the oversimplified idea among educators that in kindergarten through 3rd grade, children are learning to read, whereas in grades 4 through 12 children are reading to learn (Chall, Jacobs, & Baldwin, 1990; Chall & Jacobs, 2003). A myth circulated in the United States that teaching reading is primarily the responsibility of teachers in kindergarten through 3rd grade. Fourth-grade teachers could turn their attention to other academic tasks. Research has now shown that children should be simultaneously and continuously learning to read and reading to learn from preschool through middle school (Robb, 2011).

Both the 2009 reading framework of the National Assessment of Educational Progress and the Common Core State Standards require students to read a high and increasing proportion of informational text as they advance through the grades. What is going on? The goal of the Common Core State Standards, introduced with great fanfare in 2010 by the National Governors Association and the Council of Chief State School Officers, is making sure that high school graduates are provided the skills and knowledge they need to succeed. Yet, the new standards for student achievement in English language arts and mathematics were announced without practical plans for providing teachers with the needed professional development to effectively teach the mandated skills (Greenfader & Brouillette, 2017). As a result, states that have adopted the Common Core standards and those that have not faced similar challenges to ones encountered before in effectively helping students learn to read.

This chapter is divided into two sections. The first part focuses on close reading, a skill emphasized by the CCSS but has broad importance, independent of the Common Core standards. The second section focuses on grasping the specialized language and complex grammar of science, technology, engineering, and mathematics (STEM) texts. This is the sort of informational reading widely required at the university level and for well-paying jobs in the increasingly STEM-oriented labor market of the United States.

USING THE ARTS TO TEACH CLOSE READING

The Common Core State Standards in English language arts focus heavily on close reading and questions that elicit text-dependent responses from students in upper elementary school. Students must cite evidence from the text to justify each observation they make about what they have read. But teaching students in grades 3–5 (who may still be struggling with decoding skills) how to analyze text can be difficult. One way to simplify this task is to first show students how to analyze works of visual art, using strategies that closely resemble those specified in the Common Core standards that address the reading of informational text.

The first three CCSS standards for reading informational text, titled "Key Ideas and Details," ask students to figure out *what* a text says by explicitly referring to its words as the basis for their comments. The next three standards, titled "Craft and Structure," require students to reread the text and focus on *how* the author communicated his or her message. Again, students must explicitly cite sections of the text as the basis for their comments. The last three standards, titled "Integration of Knowledge and Ideas," call for students to decipher what the text means *within a larger context*, taking into account new clues and relating them to the text.

For a 3rd-grader, this three-part exercise can be confusing. So, the J. Paul Getty Museum's Education Department developed a set of helpful arts integration resources, now available on its YouTube channel. Most relevant is a technique termed Developing Common Core Habits (Getty Museum, 2015), described by literacy specialist Jill Jackson: Teachers practice with their students how to analyze visual artworks using "close looking" techniques. Because "close looking" replaces "close reading," children can try to perform the three-part analysis without the distraction of having to decode unfamiliar words and phrases. When students initially look at a painting, the teacher simply says, "What is going on the picture? When you answer, point to specific things we can see." Next, students are invited to take a second look, focusing on why the painter might have made specific choices in elements such as perspective or color so as to elicit a particular response from viewers. Once again, the students must include details to back up their statements. Finally, the teacher asks them to give an overall response to the painting, explaining how particular components make them feel.

Before curriculum initiatives like the Getty Museum's took shape, the typical prompt given to elementary school students asked to write about a work of art was "Do you like it?" or "How does it make you feel?" These questions can be answered with barely a glance at the painting. By asking a series of questions that require students to back up their interpretations with evidence, the teacher encourages a deeper level of engagement with the work. Therefore, when the teacher finally asks students to describe their overall impression of the painting, they are able to give a much more detailed and thoughtful response. This three-part analysis, modeled on the close reading process described in the Common Core reading standards, demonstrates to students how they can analyze visual art.

Teachers also must adjust their questioning strategies. No longer do they ask only "What do you think about this?" By adding "What gave you that feeling?" teachers help students dig a little deeper and reflect on what prompted their response. Both teachers and students become accustomed to grappling with more probing questions. For this process to be effective, all students must prepare to answer each question asked. One effective approach is for the teacher to call on students randomly. That way, students who tend to be quiet in class, not raise their hands, or sit in the back of the room will have an equal chance at being called on. "Rolling the Dice for Participation" is a strategy that uses dice to determine the table and seat number of the student who will be called on next. Alternatively, each student's name can be written on a craft stick, with the sticks kept in a cup at the front of the room. When asking questions, the teacher randomly picks a stick and calls on that student.

MEETING THE CHALLENGES OF CONTENT AREA TEXTS

For students to become adept at close reading and making inferences, they must be able to understand the type of language a text uses. Many young readers have difficulty with the academic language used in science and social studies texts. Therefore, Chapters 4 and 5 emphasize strategies for boosting comprehension of such language. The specialized vocabulary of the STEM disciplines can present particular problems. The next section focuses on ways to help students comprehend science vocabulary and concepts, mindful of the Next Generation Science Standards (NGSS),[5] which provide for science a national set of standards akin to what the Common Core State Standards provide for language arts and mathematics. A consortium of 26 states developed the NGSS in partnership with the National Science Teachers Association, the American Association for the Advancement of Science, the National Research Council, and Achieve, a nonprofit.

The NGSS are based on *A Framework for K–12 Science Education* (2012) created by the National Research Council. There are three dimensions to NGSS, which give equal emphasis to scientific inquiry and engineering design. The first dimension consists of core ideas in the science and engineering disciplines. The second one entails science and engineering practices. This means that students are expected to learn content and understand the methods used by scientists and engineers. The third dimension involves crosscutting concepts, key underlying ideas that have application across all domains of science.

These NGSS dimensions provide a convenient means for integrating science with the arts via shared crosscutting concepts (such as pattern and cause and effect), which are found in both science and the arts. Similarly, the arts and the science disciplines share a focus on analytical capacities such as acute observation. The NGSS are also built on the assumption that constructing progressively more sophisticated explanations should be central to science instruction in elementary school. This leaves room for the creation of artistic metaphors that provide children with an initial grasp of concepts that are returned to and elaborated on in future lessons. Through such arts-based activities, children become comfortable with the academic language of science. Similar strategies can also be used to teach the concepts and vocabulary of social studies and mathematics.

5. Next Generation Science Standards: https://www.nextgenscience.org/

Understanding the Academic Language of Science

> Academic language is designed to be concise, precise, and authoritative. To achieve these goals, it uses sophisticated words and complex grammatical constructions that can disrupt reading comprehension and block learning. (Snow, 2010, p. 450)

The character of the academic language used in science texts is unfamiliar to students in grades 3–5, as they are accustomed to writing styles more akin to oral language forms. In contrast, the academic language of science texts features conciseness, achieved by avoiding redundancy but with a high density of information-bearing words (Snow & Uccelli, 2009). These qualities require careful attention on the part of the reader, along with an understanding of the specialized vocabulary involved. Students need help in learning academic vocabulary and processing academic language if they are to become independent learners of science (Snow, 2010). Classroom teachers recognize that teaching vocabulary is critical, but tend to focus only on the science vocabulary (bolded words in a text) and may not recognize that the definitions provided for these boldface words use general-purpose academic vocabulary that may also be unfamiliar to students. Similar problems arise in social studies and mathematics.

Ideally, science vocabulary is not learned through reciting scripted definitions but by communicating conceptual and procedural knowledge, questions, and propositions. This is optimally done through discussion (with the whole class, or in small groups or dyads) that includes evidence-based dialogue and the use of scientific terms. Yet, students' limited knowledge of science, though, can make such discussions difficult. An alternative strategy is to design arts-based activities in which students are motivated to use science vocabulary in ways that demonstrate their understanding of the concepts represented.

Connecting the Arts to Science

The concept behind the Next Generation Science Standards is the idea that learning is a developmental progression. Therefore, the framework is designed to help children continually build on and revise their skills and knowledge, starting with their curiosity about what they see around them and their initial conceptions about how the world works. The goal is for educators to guide students' understanding in the direction of a more empirically based and coherent view of science and engineering. Well-designed arts integration lessons provide elementary school students with experiences that enable them to reach developmentally appropriate, evidence-based conclusions. The science and dance lesson described below is an example of how, through creative movement, children can gain new insights. This lesson follows up on an earlier science lesson and was designed to check—and deepen—student understanding of how time of day relates to the position of the sun in the sky.

Using Movement to Aid Visualization. A 3rd-grade teacher stood at the front of the room, backed by a construction paper representation of the sun. The children faced their teacher, standing in rows an arm's length apart. The teacher started playing a recording of soft, slow music. Then the children, each pretending to be the Earth, followed the teacher in rotating slowly, in a counterclockwise direction, to the music. When the children again directly faced the "sun," the teacher paused the music and asked, "If you were on the surface of the Earth, looking up at the sun directly overhead, what time would it be?" Children looked at her quizzically. She reminded them of their science lesson showing that, when the sun is directly above, it is noon (Graham & Brouillette, 2016). The children smiled and nodded.

The music and movement continued. When the children faced directly away from the sun, the teacher paused the music again and asked, "Can you see the sun?" "No," they replied. "Now it is midnight. You are facing away from the sun. But did the sun move?" No. Then the teacher posed a new challenge: "Rotate to the position you would be facing at 6:00 A.M. That's halfway between midnight and noon." She modeled moving a quarter turn and explained, "As we keep on rotating, notice how you can see the sun better. That means the light is getting brighter." When they arrived again at "noon," they stopped to predict what would happen to their ability to see the sun as they rotated toward 6:00 P.M. and midnight. Afterward, they practiced rotating to specific times of day.

To test students' understanding, the teacher had 12 children join hands in a circle, facing outward so their backs were toward the center of the circle. The circle rotated slowly in a counterclockwise direction. When the teacher stopped the music, the children were each in a different position in relation to the sun. So, they each "experienced" a different "time of day." With the teacher's help and their memory of their individual practice in rotating to noon, 6:00 P.M., midnight, and 6:00 A.M., the children figured out what time it would be at the spot each one was "standing" on the Earth's surface. Finally, the teacher gave every second child a badge, marked "California," "New York," "England," "Egypt," "India," or "Japan." This time, when the music stopped, the teacher asked the class what time they thought it would be at the place named on each badge. The teacher mentioned having recently passed through an airport with a row of clocks on the wall that showed the current time in cities around the world.

Although, during the science lesson the class had already talked about the relationship between the position of the sun and the time of day, these

3rd-graders remained in what Piaget (1954) referred to the "concrete operational" stage of cognitive development. This stage starts in children at approximately 7 years of age, marking the beginning of logical or operational thought. At this age, a student is mature enough to use logical rules but can apply logic only to physical objects (hence the use of the term *concrete*). Until they reach the age of 11, students typically have difficulty applying logic abstractly (without visible cues). That causes problems when they are asked to apply logic to abstract concepts in the manner of adult scientists. Therefore, concrete activities like the one described can be effective in aiding students in the intermediate grades in envisioning how the Earth's rotation determines the time of day.

Deeper Learning of Fewer Concepts. The NGSS Framework purposely focuses on a limited number of core ideas, within and across the STEM disciplines, to provide more time to explore concepts in depth. This avoids shallow coverage that lacks conceptual grounding. The emphasis on giving students a thorough conceptual grounding is rooted in research on scientific misconceptions. Even college graduates who have taken all the required science courses often harbor scientific misconceptions. A famous example can be seen in the film *A Private Universe* (Harvard-Smithsonian Center for Astrophysics, 1987), in which new Harvard graduates are unable to explain what causes the seasons. Instead, they echo a common misconception, that the Earth is closer to the sun in the summer than in the winter.

Chapter 1 describes Einstein's ability to envision, through carefully constructed thought experiments, scientific phenomena that had heretofore been difficult to understand. In upper elementary school, teachers whose science curriculum includes the cause of the seasons take on a similar challenge: helping students envision a phenomenon they cannot directly "see." How might teachers help a student who holds this misconception about the cause of seasons realize that it is mistaken?

One strategy relies on drama, with students playing roles that put them a situation where they will naturally encounter aspects of the phenomenon they are investigating. In the article "Heroes on a Learning Adventure" (2017), Heather Wolpert-Gawron explained how this strategy works. The objective is to have students participate in the project as they would in a great story. The teacher decides the following: Who are the characters? What are they trying to accomplish? What is the setting? What aspects of the project are likely to intrigue students?

Before starting the astronomy unit, a teacher in the United States might assign students to create a brief outline of a weeklong vacation they might take in New Zealand (or to the United States, if the school is in the Southern Hemisphere). A clip from *The Lord of the Rings* trilogy may be used to introduce students to the spectacular New Zealand scenery. Half the class will plan their trip for July and the other half in December. They look up the average temperature for the month they will arrive and decide what activities they will include (visiting the beach? traversing ski slopes?). What sights would they like to see? Students are given a short time to do online research.

Students write a brief outline of the planned trip, working around the real-life fact that when it is winter in the Northern Hemisphere, it is summer in the Southern Hemisphere. That introduces an element of mystery, stimulating student interest in the upcoming science unit about the seasons. This is an opportune time to show a brief clip from *A Private Universe* (Harvard-Smithsonian Center for Astrophysics, 1987) and discuss common misconceptions. The clip can be followed by an introductory discussion delving into students' own experiences so as to highlight connections between information that students already know and seasonal change.

Connecting to Personal Experience. If the misconception highlighted in *A Private Universe* were true—that the Earth really is considerably closer to the sun in summer—then the Northern and the Southern hemispheres would experience summer at the same time. Yet, that is clearly not true. What other possibilities are there? Exploring alternatives provides a chance to connect familiar facts (days are longer in summer) with new vocabulary (*solstice, equinox*) and turn student attention to the cause of such phenomena. Examination of a visual depiction of the Earth's tilted axis of rotation can not only help students envision how that tilt causes the seasons but also connect it to the midsummer "midnight sun" in the Arctic and Antarctic (where summer starts in December). Showing a clip from *The March of the Penguins* could be an effective way to provide students with a stark image of midwinter in Antarctica.

Of course, this is only an introduction to the actual science lesson. The impact of variations in the angle at which the sun's rays hit the Earth's surface (due to the tilt of the Earth's axis) will require more explanation. But such discussions can awaken student interest and point them toward a satisfying answer to the puzzle of the seasons. In the process, students may experience "aha!" moments that awaken interest in further exploration.

USING THE ARTS TO SCAFFOLD SCIENCE LESSONS

The lesson in which 3rd-graders pretended to be the Earth rotating on its axis was created as part of a 3-year project in STEAM (STEM + Art = STEAM). Arts integration strategies were used to scaffold science learning in grades 3 through 5. During the first year a school participated in the program, teaching artists made weekly visits to each classroom, co-teaching a 50-minute integrated science and arts lesson with the teacher. In the second year, classroom teachers taught the lessons themselves with support from the district's resource teachers. The lessons supplemented the science curriculum that the district had adopted for grades 3 through 5, the Full Option Science System (FOSS), which had been developed by the Lawrence Hall of Science at the University of California–Berkeley.

FOSS kits had helped elementary schools in the district's affluent neighborhoods boost science achievement. But a large gap had opened up between science achievement at schools in affluent neighborhoods and at those in less affluent neighborhoods where many of the students were English language learners (ELLs). In an effort to both close the science achievement gap and bring more arts instruction into schools in low-income neighborhoods, the California Department of Education funded a proposal that would (1) use the visual and performing arts to aid students to better understand science concepts and (2) help students become more comfortable using the science vocabulary in the FOSS science kits.

The first step was to determine which concepts students most frequently missed on the school district's benchmark tests in recent years. Then educators designed creative movement lessons to correct misconceptions and clarify concepts that students had struggled with. Physical science was targeted first because this was the discipline where students had the greatest trouble envisioning the phenomena explored in the science lessons. A quasi-experimental study was carried out to investigate the effect of nine STEAM lessons on physical science achievement in grades 3 through 5 (Graham & Brouillette, 2016). The results showed that, with other factors being equal, after students were assigned a teacher well trained in the STEAM curriculum, students in the treatment group moved from the 50th percentile to the 63rd percentile on district benchmark tests.

What Do STEAM Lessons Look Like?

As Ainsworth, Prain, and Tytler (2011) pointed out, visualization is integral to scientific thinking. Scientists do not just use words; they rely on diagrams, graphs, videos, photographs, and other images to make discoveries, explain findings, and excite public interest. Scientists imagine new relationships, test ideas, and elaborate on concepts through visual representations. In keeping with this tradition, the visual art lessons focused on science notebooks and encouraged students to look closely at natural objects, with the goal of improving their observation skills. The careful sketches students made in their notebooks while working with the science kits caused them to observe closely and keep an accurate record of their work. For teachers, the student drawings were a powerful means of picking up on misconceptions, giving teachers the opportunity to address false impressions in the following lesson.

Yet, according to teacher reports, dance and creative movement proved to be the most powerful arts tool for helping students envision phenomena that cannot easily be physically observed. The physical involvement required by dance was especially effective in getting students to (1) actively focus on the lesson and (2) transform the conceptual information contained in science lessons into a memorable personal experience. These teacher reports were in line with Kress's (2009) research on science learning, especially his description of classrooms as semiotic spaces where meaning-making occurs across modes ranging from visual and written to spoken and gesture. As Kress (2009) noted, "the world of meaning is multimodal" (p. 19).

Making Concepts Memorable Through Music and Movement

In Western culture, many children learn the letters of the alphabet as a song, set to the melody of "Twinkle, Twinkle, Little Star" (Levitin, 2008). Even as adults, we may remember the months with 30 days by repeating the rhyme "Thirty days has September. . . . " Such "knowledge songs" are a remnant of what was, for preliterate societies, a critical method of remembering and passing on knowledge. Simple singsong rhymes served as the repository of cultural knowledge, history, and day-to-day procedures for skinning an animal, making a spear, or crafting a water jug. The mutually reinforcing aspects of song lyrics—rhyme, rhythm, melody, accent structure, and alliteration—aid people in recalling musically encoded information.

> The ancient Hebrews set the entire Torah—the first five books of the Old Testament—to melody and recalled it from memory for more than a thousand years before they ever wrote it down. Even today, many Orthodox rabbis can sing every word by heart. (Levitin, 2008, p. 153)

The STEAM lessons described below incorporate this technique for helping children recall and retain the concepts and vocabulary they covered in their science lessons.

Earth Science. In a 4th-grade life science unit on ecosystems, students had set up and monitored a freshwater aquarium with different kinds of fish, plants, and other organisms. Students watched for feeding interactions among these populations. In this way, they learned about the role of producers, consumers, and decomposers in food chains. Rap-like songs were used to review concepts about ecosystems. Before presenting the rap in its final form, the class practiced the words for 5 minutes each day, for 3 days.

Their first rap goes like this:

> Small as a puddle or large as the sea, living and nonliving thrive in harmony. Animals, plankton, water, soil, air. Ecosystems are everywhere!

Once students had memorized the words, they learned the movements that went with them. Video recordings captured the teaching artists' gestures as they led lessons, so teachers could recall how the words and movements fit together. The lesson plans and videos are now available online, free of charge.[6]

Life Science. The 5th-grade life science lessons focused on the organs of the body. New vocabulary words gained conceptual meaning as children began using them in a meaningful context. This lesson required a room large enough so that a simplified version of the human circulatory system could be mapped out on the floor with painter's tape. Students, playing the role of blood cells, followed the taped pathway, chanting, "Left from the heart, away through the arteries" as they energetically exited (dancing) from the left side of the heart through the aorta. Later, as they returned through the veins to the right side of the heart, they chanted, "Right to the heart, the veins, the veins." To show the depletion of oxygen in the blood cells resulting in a loss of energy, the students drooped their shoulders as they made their way back to the heart.

The heart then pumped the blood cells to the lungs, where they became re-energized. Students who represented the lungs gave an "oxygen" card to the blood cells. Returning to the heart, the blood cells were again pumped into the rest of the body, where they gave up their "oxygen" card and took a "carbon dioxide" card. Lesson 2 in this unit depicted the activity of the digestive system. Lesson 3 showed how the circulatory system picked up nutrients from the digestive system, distributed the nutrients through the body, and brought back waste materials to be disposed of (Graham & Brouillette, 2016). During the 5th-grade life science lessons, students let out a few sheepish giggles as students made mental connections between the anatomic parts they imitated and their own bodies' workings. Finding this connection made these lessons inherently interesting.

Physical Science. The 4th-grade arts integration lesson "Get Your Motor Running: Circuits and Motors" reviewed the concepts students had explored while carrying out a science experiment on magnetism and electricity. The objective was to (1) represent (to students who were still concrete thinkers) difficult-to-describe concepts in words that all 9-year-olds know and (2) discuss these concepts, which had been difficult for students

6. Videos: https://sites.ucl.edu/teachingartistproject/

to envision. The teacher started with a quick review, saying, "In the last lesson, we saw that electric energy flows from point A to point B in a pathway. Today we give a name to that pathway. It is called a circuit."

During the warm-up segment, students reviewed their last STEAM lesson, which called on them to play the role of electrons. Dancing in a conga line, the electrons moved out of the negative pole of a "D-cell battery" (outlined by masking tape on the floor), then moved along a "wire" (also suggested by tape) to the positive pole, where they re-entered the D cell. After the review, the teacher selected a student volunteer to represent the battery's switch. This student stood between the positive pole of the D cell and the wire; that way, the switch could easily turn the electric current on and off.

Next, the students learned two short chants. The words for the "Closed Circuit Chant" were: "The switch is on; the circuit is closed; electricity flows." The chant was accompanied by a gesture: With their hands clasped in front of their bodies, the students made a circle with their arms at chest height. The words for the "Open Circuit Chant" were: "The switch is off; the circuit is open; electricity stops." While reciting this chant, students separated their hands. Then they bent their elbows and raised their lower arms to a vertical position. The student who played the switch signaled the on and off positions by using one of these gestures and saying the Open Circuit Chant or the Closed Circuit Chant. The rest of the group (except for a few students playing "electrons") said the chant and performed the gestures with the "switch." The students playing the electrons danced along the wire when the switch was closed and stopped when it was open.

Once the students could perform these actions smoothly, the teacher inserted another "wire" (indicated by tape) between the positive pole of the D cell and the switch. Then a "light bulb" (a student volunteer) stood between the positive pole of the D cell and the new wire. When electricity flowed, the "light bulb" made flashing movements with his or her arms to show the current's flow, and when the electricity stopped, he or she paused. After this representation of a simple circuit with a light bulb and a switch, the teacher posed questions for discussion, probing to see if students' understood the concepts taught in the science lesson and reviewed that day: What was causing the bulb to light up? What does the bulb do in a circuit? What is the role of the switch?

The lesson was based on Eisner's (2002) observation that humans learn by forming representations of their experiences. Students' experience of visualizing electrons flowing through a circuit enabled them to stabilize that image in their minds so they remembered it. Then they could proceed to play out various possible situations in their imagination, allowing them to anticipate when the light bulb would go on—or would not. By discussing their depiction of open and closed circuits, they expanded their scientific and academic vocabulary.

Teacher Focus Groups

The participating teachers later expressed in focus groups their enthusiasm about the experience of co-teaching STEAM lessons with a teaching artist at their school. They found this a more effective professional development exercise than after-school workshops or meetings held away from their school sites. Teachers spoke of the benefits of giving students a "double dose" of learning, starting with the science kit investigations and following up with the arts-based review lessons. They said giving students a chance to learn the same concept in different ways was especially beneficial for those whose limited academic vocabulary made it difficult to follow the discussion at the end of a science kit unit. Because the arts lessons got students up and moving, even the often restless ones became more attentive. A typical observation from teachers was: "The different learning style engaged kids who might not participate normally."

The feedback from these teachers was in line with the Dana Consortium finding that interest in a performing art leads to a high state of motivation, resulting in the sustained attention necessary to improve performance (Gazzaniga, 2008). In addition, teachers' comments echoed findings from a study in the same district that showed arts integration boosted student engagement (Brouillette, Childress-Evans, Hinga, & Farkas, 2014) and supported development of a greater sense of community within the classroom (Brouillette, 2010).

Possibilities to Consider

- Might students' difficulty in comprehending science texts be partly a result of not understanding the academic language involved?
- Do students have trouble envisioning the complex processes covered in lessons on life science, Earth science, and physical science?
- Could it help to use a playful approach like turning vocabulary words into rap lyrics or using dance to mimic the functions of the circulatory system?

A CRUCIAL DIMENSION OF STEAM

Adopting the arts as a vehicle for presenting STEM concepts can make a significant contribution to boosting the scientific knowledge of struggling students in upper elementary school. Drawing, painting, and dancing can provide children who are not yet abstract thinkers (Inhelder & Piaget, 1958) with concrete methods for envisioning phenomena that they cannot directly observe. The arts, like mathematics, may have a dual role in education. Academics already recognize mathematics as a scholarly discipline in its own right as well as a crucial tool in scientific research. Now there is growing recognition that, in STEAM projects, the arts not only play their traditional content area role but also scaffold the teaching of science concepts by representing concepts that students could not otherwise envision.

Teachers touched on a key issue when they mentioned that during STEAM lessons, there was a "wide awake" quality to their students as they worked with teaching artists that—along with the concrete nature of the activities—made it easier for them to absorb new concepts and vocabulary. This combination of motivation and developmental appropriateness may be the "missing link" that has been overlooked by scholars, who argued instead that students should be taught to understand science concepts as adult scientists do. The Next Generation Science Standards have overturned that assumption by asserting that teachers should start with children's curiosity about the world around them and their initial conceptions about how it works, then help students continually build on and revise their current knowledge and skills.

If educators aim to guide students to appreciate a more coherent and scientifically based view of how the world works, well-designed arts integration lessons can play an important role by providing students in upper elementary school experiences that enable them to reach developmentally appropriate, evidence-based conclusions. Participation in STEAM lessons and other kinds of arts integration can lead to individual cognitive growth, enhanced observation, and a deeper understanding of the world. This not only enriches individual lives but may eventually have a spillover effect, leading to an increase in overall student achievement (McCarthy, Ondaatje, Zakaras, & Brooks, 2004).

Examples of lesson plans, videos, resources, and teaching materials mentioned in this chapter may be accessed at the following website: http://sites.uci.edu/educ104donline/

CHAPTER 5

Building Effective Oral Communication Skills

> Building and maintaining a nation state has long been a precarious undertaking in the United States. . . . Disparate peoples, and their different customs that give shape to and have shaped the nation's past, present opportunities for conflict at almost every turn. (VanSledright, 2008, p. 111)

The motto "E Pluribus Unum," which appears on the Great Seal of the United States, suggests the emergence of a single nation from individuals of diverse origin. Yet, the character of the nation that emerged from this mixture of cultures remains the subject of continuing debate. Ideals like safeguarding the rights of individual citizens continue to exist in tension with other requirements, such as the need to build a national community whose citizens feel a sense of connection with one another and a respect for shared norms of responsible citizenship (VanSledright, 2008). Traditionally, helping students comprehend this complexity has been the role of the social studies curriculum. However, in recent years, a strong focus on raising achievement in English language arts and math has cut into the time spent on social studies.

Might integrating social studies concepts into literacy and arts lessons repair this intrusion and amend the gap? Historically, many of the symbols that have become emblematic of the United States were created by artists and musicians. The Statue of Liberty, the monuments in Washington, and songs like "America the Beautiful" and "Stars and Stripes Forever" inspire a sense of national pride that ideally transcends political parties. In his poem "I Hear America Singing," Walt Whitman provided a powerful metaphor for the essential individuality of each person (regardless of the groups they belong to), likening it to a distinctive "carol" that also becomes an element in a great chorus:

> I hear America singing, the varied carols I hear;
> Those of mechanics—each one singing his, as it should be, blithe and
>   strong

The delicious singing of the mother, or of the young wife at work . . .
Each singing what belongs to him or her, and to none else. (Whitman,
2002)

Whitman's metaphor provides the theme for this chapter. The Common Core anchor standards for speaking and listening state that students must have ample opportunities to take part in a variety of rich, structured conversations—as part of a whole class, in small groups, and with a partner. Such conversations are recommended for students in the earliest grades. Yet, given the limited vocabulary and background knowledge of young children, forethought is needed, especially when some of the children in the class are English language learners. About 4.8 million children in the schools of the United States have limited English proficiency and are designated as English language learners (NCES, 2018). The next section explores theater activities in a 1st-grade classroom with many children who speak mostly Spanish at home, and looks at hows oral interaction was encouraged in class. Teaching artists from the San Diego Guild of Puppetry taught a series of eight puppetry workshops, in which children experimented with playing a wide range of roles.

LEARNING ORAL COMMUNICATION SKILLS THROUGH PUPPETRY

When participating in puppet theater, any student can play any role, without limitations related to size, age, gender, ethnic origin, or physical or verbal ability (Brouillette & Jennings, 2010). All that matters is a child's ability to imagine and create a believable character, then bring it to life. This flexibility lets a child puppeteer explore different roles and what it is like to walk in another's shoes. Students frequently behave differently when performing puppet theater than they do the rest of the school day. A shy child may happily portray a bold, brash character, while a student with difficulty keeping still in class may focus intently on manipulating a puppet so as to portray a slow-moving, timid character.

During one 1st-grade theater workshop, children sat on the carpet, attentively watching a teaching artist who stood next to the puppet stage. The puppeteer explained, "These black sweatshirts and black gloves are what you will be wearing when your puppets perform onstage. Why do you think you would want to wear black while performing?" The children looked puzzled. "Raise your hand if you would like to try on the black sweatshirt and gloves," the teaching artist said. A boy raised his hand.

The teaching artist continued, "Watch when I put the puppet in front of Franklin when he is wearing black. What do you see?" The puppet! cried the children. "So the audience sees the puppet and doesn't notice the puppeteer when you are wearing black," the artist noted. Children grinned at the thought of disappearing. The puppeteers then presented the story of the "Three Billy Goats Gruff." Then they asked who wanted to help present the puppet play. Children raised their hands and eagerly volunteered for various roles.

Although many of the children in that class spoke Spanish at home, the wide range of English proficiency among them is not readily apparent to a casual onlooker. During the puppetry activities, there is always a rewarding role for each child to play. Although not all children felt confident that day about playing a major onstage role, the need for sound effects and scenery presented other options. Musicians with rhythm instruments sat beside the stage and complemented the movement of the puppets. As the littlest goat crossed the stage, a child used a tortoiseshell and stick to create the sound of small goat steps. When the medium-size goat crossed the stage, a child tapped a small drum to create the sound of his medium-size steps.

On a social–emotional level, the most important element of the workshop was the imaginative engagement of all class members. When imagining the hopes and fears of famished goats trying to cross a bridge guarded by a hungry troll, the children brought their own life experiences, abilities, desires, wishes, and dreams. Whatever their level of facility with oral English, all these human attributes were already in place when the children walked into the classroom. The puppetry workshop simply tapped into these resources. If a child did not know the right words, the puppeteer coached him or her, rephrased the question, or suggested part of an appropriate response.

The puppetry workshop not only encouraged but required that children interact with one another and use language in a variety of ways. This instilled confidence. At the beginning of the year, when teachers asked children a question, they often responded with only one or two words. But over time, these students learned to provide more detail and precision in their answers. As they became more comfortable with discussion and volunteered longer responses, their language skills improved. In this sense, the puppetry workshops provided a safe, yet risk-taking environment. Children gained confidence by trying new things. One benefit the children gained from taking these risks was the development of enhanced communication skills.

INTRODUCING CHILDREN TO SOCIAL STUDIES

The introduction to this chapter touches on challenges the United States has faced in forging a single nation out of individuals of diverse origin. Helping students comprehend this complexity has been the role of the social studies curriculum (Schneider et al., 1994). The Common Core standards provide an opportunity to also address social studies concepts within the literacy curriculum. The National Council for the Social Studies (1994) explained:

> The primary purpose of social studies is to help young people make informed and reasoned decisions for the public good as citizens of a culturally diverse, democratic society in an interdependent world. (p. 3)

Evidence suggests that the social studies curriculum has not been effective in reaching this goal, however. Two key areas within social studies are geography and history. On the 2014 National Assessment of Academic Progress (2015), often described as the nation's report card, only 27% of U.S. 8th-graders performed at or above the proficient level in geography. Just 18% performed at or above that level in U.S. history. These results may be related to the amount of time children and teens now spend on texting, videogames, and social media accounts. Dr. Elias Aboujaoude, director of the Stanford University Impulse Control Disorders Clinic, made the following assertion:

> The more we become used to just sound bites and tweets, the less patient we will become with more complex, more meaningful information. And I do think we might lose the ability to analyze things with any depth and nuance. Like any skill, if you don't use it, you lose it. (Evangelista, 2009)

If the focus of the social studies curriculum is on civic competence—the knowledge, intellectual processes, and democratic dispositions required for students to become active and engaged participants in public life—then educators should look for indications of whether progress is being made toward this goal. Is there evidence within the general population of an increased disposition to respect the rights of fellow citizens and interact with them in a civil manner? A survey by NORC (2016) at the University of Chicago found that 74% of the Americans it polled said the manners and behavior of their fellow citizens have deteriorated in recent decades. Technology addiction appears to be a factor, as it tends to cause diminished interest in offline, face-to-face interactions. According to the Pew Research Center (2018), more than 95% of teens have access to a smartphone; 45% say that they are online "almost constantly."

This increased focus on electronic communication is taking place at a time when advanced face-to-face social skills are in great demand in the workplace. Employment in jobs requiring average or above-average levels of interpersonal, communications, or management skills increased 83% from 1980 to 2015; whereas employment in jobs requiring higher levels of analytical skills, such as critical thinking and computer use, increased 77% (Pew Research Center, 2016). Perhaps the concerted push in recent years to prepare students for a job market that puts a premium on digital skills has ignored something more basic: the continuing need for non-screen-based communication skills. The next section looks at how teachers might help broaden students' understanding of social issues by integrating age-appropriate historical works into the literacy curriculum.

Exploring Geography and History

Reading and writing float on a sea of talk. (James Britton, 1982, p. 11)

By the time they reach 3rd grade, children have gained sufficient background knowledge and mastery of oral language to meaningfully discuss questions such as these: Who were the first people to live in my community? How did they come here? How has my community changed over time? What issues are important to my community? Historical accounts of the development of other communities can be a good place to start. *A River Ran Wild* by Lynne Cherry (2002) tells a powerful story of human–environment interaction, explaining how descendants of the Nash-a-way tribe and European settlers in recent decades have taken actions to address industrial pollution and restore the natural beauty of the Nashua River in Massachusetts. Although the book is set in a specific locale, it focuses on issues encountered in many communities. Teachers may wish to focus on discussing the examples of cause and effect found throughout the book. Such discussions could easily be extended to cover local issues relating to human–environment interaction and what is being done to safeguard the local area's water, air, and open spaces.

Other books also can demonstrate to students the importance of geography in shaping the way people settled a community. Bonnie and Arthur Geisert have created a fascinating genre of picture books, including *Prairie Town* (1998), *River Town* (1999), *Mountain Town* (2000), and *Desert Town* (2001). Each book presents life in a specific geographic environment, largely through pictures, with spare text. For example, *Prairie Town* uses full-page illustrations that provide details about the economic and social interdependence of people in a Midwestern town in the early 1900s with surrounding farms. Children can follow the community's life through the seasons, by reading about the spring plowing, harvesting the grain in the summer, the reopening of school, burning fallen leaves in the fall, and enduring a winter blizzard. A teacher can challenge the students with this question: How much can you see in the illustrations? After reading the book aloud, a teacher may divide the class into groups, with students competing to see who discovers the most details by studying the illustrations when they have finished other assignments. Careful observers will notice many particulars of town life, like a marriage, a traffic ticket, and an expansion of a tree house. Groups can then take turns presenting details they have discovered to the class, dropping out of the competition when they have run out of new details.

River Town has a sharper economic focus, showing how in the 18th and 19th centuries people formed towns along rivers where fur trappers built trading posts or ferries crossed the water. Trucks, trains, and barges carried away the town's goods, as well as produce from surrounding farms. Again, use of an exploratory approach encourages students to study the intricate drawings in their free time, allowing them to make intriguing discoveries on their own and share these with peers. Teachers may also wish to expand on this from a literacy perspective, pointing out how the text and illustrations support one another and noting that illustrators make many decisions about their pictures for the same reasons writers make decisions about words (Ray, 2010). A similar approach may be used with the bilingual picture book *My Diary from Here to There* by Amada Irma Pérez (2009), which recounts the move of a family from Mexico to Southern California for economic reasons. Here, the focus is on the push-pull factors behind decisions to move to a new area. But in place of participating in a contest, the class may engage in a discussion about what brought people to their local area.

Researchers have shown that peer discussion of academic content enhances student understanding, even when none of the students in the discussion group initially knows the correct answer (Smith et al., 2009). This supports the constructivist view that students can arrive at conceptual understanding on their own, through a process of group discussion and debate. Later in the chapter we will discuss how a child's justifying his or her explanation to another student and examining peers' explanations can develop both communication skills and content area expertise. This creates the possibility for a deeper understanding of social studies content.

Realizing the Importance of Community

In our high-tech era, students can find it difficult to envision the daily lives of people in a preindustrial age. Teachers can awaken interest by posing some concrete questions: You have seen pictures of log cabins. But what steps would one have to go through to make one without machinery of the type we have today? What kinds of trees would have the straight, sturdy trunks needed? Once logs were cut into the size and shape required, how would they be lifted into place? By brainstorming possible answers to these questions, students begin to envision the kinds of problems early

European settlers grappled with. After this discussion, the teacher can suggest that the culture of frontier communities could have been a key factor. Even now, some communities exhibit similar cultural norms. A video of an Amish barn raising, carried out by the whole community, could provide insight into the crucial importance of community cohesion in colonial America. A barn raising was a community event at which all members of a community pitched in.

Outside of Amish communities, the custom of barn raising has faded in the United States. Building methods have changed. Urbanization has disrupted the cooperative ethic required for such endeavors. But in colonial America, the community expected all members to help out, with the understanding that the favor could be returned if need be in the future. Back then, this was the closest thing to an insurance policy anyone had. Yet people also looked forward to barn raisings, because they had the character of a festival. Men worked. Women cooked. Children played. This combination of work and celebration is well portrayed in a scene within the 1985 film *Witness*.[7]

Of course, a barn raising would be impossible to reproduce in the classroom, but other tasks requiring close collaboration can provide insight into the mindset needed. The centuries-old tradition of using tuned sets of handbells to play melodies is fun for children and has been made budget-friendly by the manufacture of inexpensive, color-coded bells. The deeper lesson conveyed is about an aspect of communication that extends beyond words: Close attention to another person's movements makes it possible to act as one or "in concert."

Creating a Handbell Ensemble

Participating in a coordinated effort to produce a recognizable song—with each person playing just one or two notes—allows students to experience the elation of participating in a complex yet fruitful group activity. A handbell ensemble acts as one instrument, with each student responsible for a particular note (or notes). Modern handbell sets for children can be color-coded, enabling students to quickly learn to read color-coded musical scores. Since the bells are played standing, students are physically active, boosting engagement. The whole group, working together, creates the song, building camaraderie. One set of bells will suffice for a whole class if students are separated into groups of four to eight (limited by the number of bells in a one-octave set). But the activity can be noisy, so it may be best for groups to practice during lunch or recess. When each group has learned a song, the class can host a performance, with one set of bells passed back and forth so that each group can play.

7. *Witness* (1985) "Building Barn": https://www.youtube.com/watch?v=BL_X7GelX5Q

Afterward, students can discuss how it felt to create a song together. Were they surprised by how skilled they sounded in the end? Taking a playful approach, the teacher can furnish a Venn diagram so students can compare and contrast the characteristics of a handbell ensemble and a barn raising. Obvious differences exist, but the teacher may suggest a few key similarities. Both endeavors require a clear plan (a musical score and a building plan) and assigned tasks. Otherwise, people will not know what to do. Participants must also be aware of what others are doing and adjust their actions so as to achieve the best final result. Otherwise the whole undertaking may fall apart. This makes a participant's attitude important, along with respect for the contributions of others.

HOW MUSIC BUILDS RAPPORT

> I can sit down and listen to the music made by Inuit Eskimos or Amazonians, and to an extent I can engage with that music. I can enjoy it. I can understand it. I can feel the same emotions they do. I can enter into their musical world. And yet, if I listen to them speak, I have no idea what they are speaking about. (Mithen, 2005)

Archeologist Steven Mithen's experience of listening to the music of indigenous groups was similar to that of English speakers who enjoy listening to Italian opera even though they speak no Italian. The emotional and neurological dimensions of music appear to extend beyond the limits of language. Why? Humans' shared biological heritage might account for this. A human fetus begins to hear 17 to 19 weeks after conception (Mannes, 2011). Without light to see, the fetus lives in a world of heartbeats, rhythm, and vibration. In hospitals, the connection of music to the body is used to steady the breathing of premature babies. When a person says, "That piece of music touched me" or "That song moved me," the experience he or she describes is quite visceral. Sound enters the ear canal and moves the eardrum. Musical vibrations literally touch the hearer. Yet, once the vibrations cease, the music is gone. For someone to hear the same music again, the sound must be re-created. The transitory nature of music gives an individual's response special intensity.

Research on music highlights similarities—rooted in humans' physical and psychological makeup—in the experiences that bring human beings pleasure, not only across cultures but across time. Bone flutes found by archeologist Nicholas Conard and his colleagues have been dated at 35,000 years old, according to tests. Copies of these flutes have been made and played. "The scale these flutes play is very similar to what is produced by flutes made today, perhaps evidence that our human preference for certain intervals is very old" (Mannes, 2011, p. 102). There may also be something unique about the way music is processed by the brain.

Some individuals with Alzheimer's disease still preserve musical memories, even when they remember little else, because key areas of the brain (linked to musical memory) have remained relatively undamaged by the illness (Graff-Radford, 2018). Thus humans' musical ability may not be simply a spin-off from language (as Steven Pinker has proposed). In *The Singing Neanderthals*, Steven Mithen (2005) speculated that humans developed a capacity for music even before they developed language. Referencing primate studies, Mithen compared group music making to grooming, an activity that evokes feelings of contentment and belonging. As humans evolved, musical vocalizations helped ensure the well-being of individuals and the cohesiveness of the group, Mithen and his colleagues hypothesized:

> The vocalizations of apes and monkeys often have a musical nature to them, heard most dramatically in the rhythmic chattering of geladas and the 'duets' 'sung' by paired gibbons. Such non-human primate calls should be described as 'holistic' because they do not appear to be composed out of discrete 'words' with their own individual meanings and which can be recombined to make novel utterances. *The Singing Neanderthals* argues that the vocalizations of our Pliocene ancestors would have been similar and these directly evolved into human language and music during the course of hominin evolution. (Mithen, Morley, Wray, Tallerman, & Gamble, 2006, p. 98)

Neuroscientist Daniel Levitin (2008) pointed out that social tension is the primary reason that nonhuman primates rarely travel in groups larger than a few dozen; their social order simply cannot be maintained in larger assemblies. Humans have overcome this limitation on group size. The question is how? Levitin has argued that synchronous, coordinated song and movement created the strongest bonds among early humans, allowing for the formation of larger living groups and eventually the societies of today.

Synchronized movement would have made collective tasks—from hauling heavy objects for building to sowing seeds with human-driven plows—much easier to undertake. Rhythmic coordination of the muscular effort involved may have been prompted, facilitated, and motivated through song, like traditional work songs, still chanted around the world today. Productive cooperation promotes feelings of togetherness, as Daniel Levitin (2008) observed:

> Consistently, across all cultures we know of, music induces, evokes, incites, and conveys emotion. This is especially true of the music in traditional societies. And in laboratories, music is probably the most reliable (nonpharmaceutical) agent we have for mood induction. (p. 146)

Music in the Continental Army

The effectiveness of synchronous, coordinated music and movement is clearly evident in the contemporary marching bands that take over the field at halftime during college football games and the large audiences drawn to television programs such as *Dancing with the Stars*. Military bands still routinely march in holiday parades, but before invention of the radio music played a crucial role in army life. Fifth-graders studying the American Revolution can gain insight into the composition of the Continental Army by analyzing scenes like those portrayed in the painting *The Spirit of '76*.[8] An old man and a boy march, playing drums, next to a wounded soldier playing a fife. The meaning of the composition, combining an old musician, a young one, and another who is wounded, may escape students unless the teacher points out that this choice is historically accurate. Patriotic males who were too old, too young, or too injured to fight did, in fact, play the fife and drum. But why?

Music played an important role in America's revolutionary days. In an era without modern communications, music helped keep order as soldiers marched to battle and helped them function well as a unit. The fife's high-pitched sound could be heard over great distances; along with the drum, it could be heard even through the sounds of battle. Whenever an officer needed to spread a command throughout the army, whether at a camp or on a battlefield, a fifer and drummer would play the tune. Then other fifers and drummers would start playing the same tune, until all soldiers knew what they needed to do. Although much more sophisticated than the calls of monkeys and primates that were referred to in the previous section, this use of sound to spread a message quickly appears to have roots far back in human history. In the Continental Army, drummers would beat out patterns that told the soldiers to turn right or left, as well as when to load and fire their muskets. In camp, music told soldiers when to wake up, eat meals, do chores, and go to bed.

Songs of the American Revolution

> We have books for political history. . . . But music is one of the most intimate expressions. Through music you become knowledgeable of the intimate aspects of life that aren't told in books. The people themselves tell you their stories—it's not an interpretation. (Henrietta Yurchenco, quoted in Handwerk, 2003)

The David versus Goliath story of colonial farmers taking on trained British troops during the American Revolution is intriguing to students.

8. *The Spirit of '76:* https://commons.wikimedia.org/wiki/File:Sprit_of_%2776.2.jpeg

Songs written in that era can help students understand the backdrop for these struggles. As Whitman suggested in "I Hear America Singing," different segments of the population had distinct perspectives, which were often expressed through song. "Yankee Doodle" was originally a British song making fun of American "doodles" (or simpletons). *Yankee* was a withering word for a colonist (Segal, 2017). The "macaroni" (the feather an American supposedly stuck in his cap) was a reference to an ostentatious subculture of British fops. Popularized by British troops during the Revolutionary War, they intended the song as an insult. The "Liberty Song" expressed the perspective of the wealthy leaders of the American Revolution. In contrast, the song "Johnny Has Gone for a Soldier" provides insight into the impact the war had on the loved ones that the revolutionary soldiers in the Continental Army had left behind.

To better understand how circumstances shaped the viewpoints of these groups, students might listen to each song, then try to imagine the backstory of the people who liked to sing it. Before hearing about a song's origins, they could jot down their best guess about experiences and social circumstances that fostered its viewpoint. Children might find the familiar strains of "Yankee Doodle" the easiest to tackle: Once the Americans started winning the war, they adopted the song as their own. So, it can be seen as English or American. After General Charles Cornwallis surrendered his British forces at Yorktown, Virginia, an English officer, Thomas Aubrey, reported, "It was not a little mortifying to hear them play this tune, when their army marched down to our surrender" (Segal, 2017).

After listening to the "Liberty Song," students could discuss the backstory of the wealthy colonial landowners and merchants who became the leaders of the American Revolution. These men risked losing their fortunes—and even their lives—to the cause of independence. Yet they also belonged to the elite social class that included George Washington, Benjamin Franklin, and John Hancock. What might have drawn people like this to the revolution?

Despite the bravery of the Founding Fathers, these men may not have been the ones who sacrificed the most in the cause of freedom. The final backstory teachers may wish to explore with their students is that of the young woman whose fate is chronicled in "Johnny Has Gone for a Soldier." This song may have been adapted from the old Irish lament "Shule Aroon" by Americans during the Revolutionary War. It echoes the universal tragedy of war. The lyrics include the following verses:

> She sold her rack, she sold her reel.
> She sold her only spinning wheel
> To buy her love a sword of steel.

Johnny has gone for a soldier.
She'll dye her dress, she'll dye it red,
And in the streets go begging for bread,
For one she loves from her has fled.
Johnny has gone for a soldier.

This young woman has sold what little she possessed to support the man she loved. Having sold her spinning wheel, this woman no longer has a way to support herself. She is forced to beg for food to keep from starving. But after the Revolutionary War, future generations of women would win greater opportunities.

Music as a Lens for Looking at Cultural Migration

With funding from the National Geographic Society Education Foundation, graduate student Stephanie Feder developed a series of lessons at the University of California–Irvine that encourage students to look more closely at musical aspects of contemporary culture, which have become so familiar that people seldom give them much thought. An example is the violin. Its English name comes from the Middle Latin *vitula*, meaning "stringed instrument," a term that also might be the source of the English word *fiddle*. The violin in its present form emerged in the early 16th century in northern Italy. But where did it originate? Examining how the violin is played provides a hint. The unique sound of the violin is produced by a horsehair bow rubbing across gut strings.

The ancestors of the violin appear to have traveled to Italy's trading cities from the steppes of Asia, where similar instruments survive today (Smithsonian Institution, 2002). In central Asia, long before the violin appeared in Italy, Turkic and Mongolian peoples fashioned two-stringed upright fiddles (similar to the Chinese *erhu*) and played them with horsehair bows. After the westward migration of the Turkic and Mongolian people brought these fiddles to the attention of Europeans, the haunting sound produced by the horsehair bow rubbing across the gut strings inspired Europeans to create their own version of the instrument. The violins, violas, and cellos found in Western orchestras today also have bows strung with horsehair. So does the fiddle, which is virtually the same instrument as the violin, except that fiddlers seldom use vibrato and most choose to set up their instrument so they can play very quickly. In the days before the advent of radio, fiddles were very popular along the American frontier.

The banjo, in contrast, resembles a drum with strings; it was modeled after instruments fashioned from hollowed-out wood or gourds. Crafted by enslaved Africans in the American South and Appalachia, early banjos had a wooden rim with a calf- or goatskin drumhead stretched across; a wooden neck mounted on the side of the rim had four or five strings and a bridge. The drumlike body of the banjo gives it a unique sound, distinct from that of the guitar, a European import whose ancestors (the lute and its relations) originated 4,000 years ago. In the early days of the United States, these three easily portable instruments—the fiddle, banjo, and guitar—accompanied a diverse group of settlers. Their intent: carving farmsteads out of the wilderness, although the steep mountain valleys proved more difficult to farm than the land along Atlantic the coast.

Prominent among them were Scottish-Irish settlers, who brought their fiddle music and ballads with them, laying the foundation for country music. The music that the Scots Irish brought with them from the British Isles often deals with the same archetypal themes of love, loss, and deception as contemporary soap operas. Before the days of television broadcasts, people commonly shared such narratives by setting them to music. Over time, these narratives became a hallmark of country music. As country music evolved, it captured the hardscrabble life and resilience of families who still lived near the mountains where their forebears had first settled.

In recent decades, the country music tradition that began in the Appalachian Mountains and became infused with African American rhythms and instruments has gained widespread popularity. Many people now perceive country music to be quintessentially American. Yet, to a historically informed observer, a country music band—including a fiddler, guitarist, and banjo player—provides a thought-provoking example of the globe-spanning traditions that shaped the culture of the United States.

Possibilities to Consider

- Do students have difficulty articulating the contributions made by immigrants from nations around the world to the building of a unique American culture?
- Is it difficult for students to relate to the horse-drawn carriage days of their state's early history as well as colonial America in general and the Revolutionary War?
- Might studying historical and ethnic songs help students to envision the lives, hopes, and concerns of people who lived in different eras and locales?

VIEWING THE PAST FROM MULTIPLE PERSPECTIVES

Instead of seeing math and science, for example, in terms of particular skills, knowledge, and manipulations, we would see them as among

the greatest of human adventures, full of drama, hopes and disap-
pointments, discoveries and inventions. (Egan, 1997, p. 64)

Kieran Egan (1997) proposed that people once again begin to regard math
and science in their proper human context. Why did the individuals who
discovered the phenomena that now fill textbooks care so passionately
about what they were doing? From the invention of pottery glazes (allowing dishes to be kept clean) to the discovery of penicillin, history is full of
breakthroughs that made an enormous difference to people at the time. By
explaining the human impact of these advances, educators can inspire students to care more about discoveries and inventions that are often treated
as mundane facts in textbooks to be memorized. Great stories need not be
fictional. Stories, after all, provide children with their initial grasp on the
world. Reimagining the school curriculum as a set of great stories to tell
children offers advantages. As the children grow, the stories could become
more complex and nuanced.

The same case can be made in the field of history. By the time they
reach 5th grade, students are becoming more interested in the abstract
ideas of liberty, loyalty, and justice, concepts that can mean different things
to different people. But a plethora of diverging perspectives need not prevent educators from investigating the causes, events, and eventual outcome
of the American Revolution. The next section examines at how 5th-graders
can learn to view events from multiple perspectives as they explore the circumstances and events that brought the United States into being.

Beyond the Good Guys Versus the Bad Guys

Following the French and Indian War of 1754 to 1763, England raised taxes
on the colonists along the Atlantic shores to recoup its costs of defend-
ing its North American colonies from the French. Tensions arose between
American colonists and British government officials, eventually bursting
into violence in 1770 with the Boston Massacre, the bloody put-down of
a riot of angry colonists, who had been taunting British troops. Differing
perspectives existed, even among colonial patriots. Silversmith Paul Revere
crafted a famous engraving immortalizing the Boston Massacre; 5 years later, he played a famous role in the resistance to British military occupation
of Boston.

What is less widely known is that when the British soldiers who had
shot and killed five colonists during the Boston Massacre went on trial,
the lawyer who successfully defended them was John Adams, a key figure
in the American Revolution and later the second president of the United
States. Actor Paul Giamatti delivers a short but powerful speech, explaining Adams's perspective, in the HBO miniseries *John Adams*: Although

Adams affirms that taxation without representation can cause men to feel abused, he presents a strong argument that the outnumbered British soldiers had reason to be afraid. He warns the jury to be careful lest, borne away by passion, they make a shipwreck of conscience. In that moment, Adams forces many in the courtroom to reconsider assumptions about what constitutes justice.

In contrast to science, whose facts can be discovered through experimentation, history depends on documents and observations that have been preserved. Historians must often contend with conflicting evidence. Inevitably, what scholars know has been influenced by the perspectives of the people who provided the documents relied on. A class discussion about whether John Adams was right to defend the British soldiers could serve as an effective way to spur students into thinking about the importance of perspective. Studying the poem "Paul Revere's Ride" may stimulate students to think more deeply about point of view.

Weighing the Impact of Poetic License

"Paul Revere's Ride" was written by Henry Wadsworth Longfellow in 1861, when the United States was on the brink of Civil War. It provides a glimpse of how some people viewed the events that led to the American Revolution almost a century later. Longfellow, a Massachusetts abolitionist, was trying to inspire a sense of patriotism and national pride right when South Carolina seceded from the United States. The poet's intent can be observed in the way the piece fluctuates between past and present tense—connecting historical and contemporary events—while communicating a sense of urgency. The poem was inspired by a visit Longfellow made to the tower of Boston's Old North Church.[9] The church's website now provides information on the poetic license Longfellow took when writing the poem. In an effort to create an American legend, Longfellow gave Revere sole credit for the achievements of three riders. Paul Revere and William Dawes rode from Boston to Lexington by different routes, warning townspeople and farmers along their way of the movement of British troops.

Revere warned colonial leaders Samuel Adams and John Hancock, who were in Lexington, of the effort to capture them. Yet British forces captured Revere while he was on his way to Concord, where the American militia's arsenal was hidden. Stephen Prescott, a Concord physician who had encountered Revere and Dawes in Lexington, was the only rider who made it to Concord to warn the militia of the approaching British troops. Teachers can raise this question with the class: Almost 250 years after the American Revolution, what should students make of this poem, which many people still assume to be an accurate account?

9. Old North Church website: https://oldnorth.com/longfellows-poem-paul-reveres-ride/

After pointing out the inaccuracies, teachers may wish to ask groups of students to create their own version of various stanzas in "Paul Revere's Ride," based on their group's preferred compromise between factual accuracy and efficiently communicating the historical significance of events. How much does it matter that Revere placed the lanterns in the church tower, not his friend? Or that other people rowed Revere across the Charles River? Would taking time to explain the separate roles of Revere, Dawes, and Prescott have reduced the impact of the poem? Or did Longfellow's simplification of the events that night undermine the story? Once students rewrite their stanzas, the teacher may substitute their stanzas for the originals and read the poem aloud. Students can then discuss the strengths and weaknesses of the original work as compared with the revised poem in terms of historical accuracy and other goals of an author. Did Longfellow's objective of abolishing slavery and preserving the Union justify his decision to change facts so as to elicit a desired emotional reaction from readers?

INTRODUCING VARIED OUTLOOKS IN K–5 SOCIAL STUDIES

What makes discussion of the poetic license exercised by Longfellow in writing "Paul Revere's Ride" challenging is that the concrete facts involved (How many riders started out from Boston? Did Revere make it all the way to Concord?) exist in a different dimension from the abstract ideals of liberty and justice. Abstract concepts cannot be seen or heard, yet they can be conveyed through emotive stories and poetry. By inspiring readers to vicariously experience what colonial patriots like Paul Revere may have thought and felt at a crucial moment in American history, Longfellow attempts to pass along their ideals. Yet, we cannot know if Longfellow's interpretation of Revere's motives is accurate.

As 5th-graders gradually construct their own understanding of the foundations of their nation, they benefit from an awareness that historical narratives are told from varied points of view. Another author might have a different perspective. Stories are a powerful way to convey abstract ideas to students who remain concrete thinkers. But presenting students with differing perspectives—such as those of John Adams and Paul Revere about the Boston Massacre—helps them build a deeper understanding of historical events. Nor is this simply a question of whose view was right or wrong; many talents were needed to build a new nation. Revere went on to fight in the Revolutionary War, while Adams ended up representing Massachusetts in the Continental Congress. Each man contributed in his own way.

Whitman's words—"I hear America singing, the varied carols I hear"— provide a useful metaphor for the alert interest in the evolution of America's culture that teachers may awaken in students by reading and discussing with them historical works such as "Paul Revere's Ride" and the poetry of African American author Phillis Wheatley. Yet, more modern works also have a contribution to make. *Johnny Tremain* (Forbes, 1943/2011), a Newbery Medal–winning novel, takes readers inside pivotal events from the Boston Tea Party and first shots at Lexington, as seen through the eyes of a young participant. The humorous classic *Ben and Me* (Lawson, 1939/1988) brings to life the many accomplishments of Benjamin Franklin, as described by fictional companion Amos the mouse. Each such book helps expand students' awareness of their nation's complex history.

Examples of lesson plans, videos, resources, and teaching materials mentioned in this chapter may be accessed at the following website: http://sites.uci.edu/educ104donline/

CHAPTER 6

Expression Through Narrative Writing

> Storytelling is a key part of our lives. When we arrive home after a
> busy day at work or school, we will tell our families in great detail
> about the events of our day. . . . We will describe and detail, exagger-
> ate and embellish and relish in our listeners' reactions to the tale we
> have told. We all tell stories every day. (Simpson, 2016)

Visual art shows how the artist perceived a scene, pointing out aspects we might have missed. Narrative adds the element of time, enabling readers to follow an incident in someone else's life as it unfolded. Stories are one of the oldest forms of teaching, establishing and renewing connections between people. Listening to stories enables humans to see the world through the eyes of another. The vicarious experiences provided by stories help children make sense of the world. Storytelling can also be a pivotal tool for helping students build their literacy skills.

Children's acquisition of narrative skills, such as storytelling and story comprehension, has been linked to scholastic success (DeTemple & Tabors, 1996). This suggests that students' literacy skills are linked to the ability to tell a story that can be understood by listeners who were not present when the events occurred. Unfortunately, research indicates that at the time children begin school, many remain unable to create sufficiently informative and well-structured narratives (Paris & Paris, 2003) to make themselves understood. Participating in educational drama and theater can promote narrative development (Mages, 2017). As discussed in Chapter 2, classroom drama provides students in early elementary school a chance to develop important skills they had not acquired before starting school.

This chapter focuses on the next step: the creation of written narratives. The strategies explored include two authors' advocacy of picture books and drawing to inspire writing in the early grades. Then we explore strategies used by teaching artists' who work in museums to help students in grades 3 through 5 build confidence as writers. Next we visit a poetry workshop at a Spanish–English dual immersion school. Finally, we watch a teaching artist share an innovative way of inspiring students to write original stories based on their own experiences.

COMBINING IMAGES AND WRITING IN THE PRIMARY GRADES

What cannot be conveyed or constructed in words is often possible in visual images or music. Becoming literate in the broadest sense means learning how to read these images. (Eisner, 1998, p. 15)

Visual art and the written word are routinely combined to convey complex ideas to children in the early grades. Through transmediation, the process of translating a work into a different medium, children's comprehension of both images and a text narrative can be significantly deepened. Beth Olshansky (2008) provides a step-by-step description of the process of picture writing. Using high-quality picture books, teachers guide children through the process of "reading the picture." Children discuss what they see and predict what might happen. Hopping back and forth between the visuals and verbal texts, children build vocabulary and comprehension; eventually, the children create their own picture books.

During their early years in school, children learn to recognize and make use of the signs and symbols of their culture. Gill Hope (2008) provided an in-depth exploration of the value (and diverse uses) of drawing in the classroom. Hope explored drawing as a container for ideas and as a journey through which ideas take shape. She cautioned adults against taking the view that a child's development as an artist should be defined in terms of creating ever more realistic representation. Instead, she encouraged adults to recognize the key conceptual leap that occurs in a young child's consciousness when drawing becomes "a portal between the inner and outer reality" (Hope, 2008, p. 67).

IMAGES AS INSPIRATION FOR WRITING

This section focuses on an innovative program that helped students in grades 3 through 5 use visual art as a prompt to become better writers. The program's inspiration came from writers in residence who worked in Houston schools with large numbers of students who speak a language other than English at home. A prominent feature of this Writing in the Museum program was its partnership with a major art museum. On mornings when the museum closed its doors to the public, about 60 children stepped off school buses. The organizers of the program divided the children into groups small enough to encourage individual participation. A writer in residence joined each group and led the students on a writing tour of the museum, which marked the high point of a semester-long program of weekly, hourlong writing workshops held at the students' school.

The Houston school district serves a diverse population, with about 46% of the children having Hispanic ancestry, 37% having an African American background, 14% identified as Anglo, and 3% as Asian. Educators developed this writing program to explore new ways to help culturally and linguistically diverse groups of students feel at ease in the unfamiliar and imposing museum building. Each writer in residence took students to view various artists' depictions of sunlit jungles, medieval peasants, and monarchs from Benin. As students walked through the galleries, their writer guide encouraged them to experience art in ways they might have been unaccustomed to. Following their creative thought patterns, the students arrived at their own conclusions. The works of art provided a road map of sorts for each writer in residence to guide the children in writing their own narratives later that day. As described in the vignette below, a playwright prepared a group of 3rd-graders for their tour by lightheartedly introducing elements of myth and story:

> "How many of you have seen pictures of a castle?" asked the playwright.
>
> A small forest of hands went up. "Well, the building in front of you is like a castle, except it doesn't have a moat and a drawbridge. But do you see how it sits, by itself, on a whole city block, with all this grass around it, and the sidewalk going all the way around the building?" said the writer, adding, "If you look through that glass door, right there, you can see a guard standing inside. He's guarding all the valuable art, just like a guard at a castle or a palace might do. In fact, it used to be that it was only in palaces that people could see the sort of art collection that we are about to see. But, before we go in, I have to tell you about the mystery."
>
> A child asked, "What mystery?"
>
> The playwright continued, "People who have seen strange things in the museum talk about an invisible princess, or maybe a prince, who may live in the museum. You see, the museum is full of beautiful art, just like a princess would have had in her castle, back when some people still lived in castles."
>
> One child let out a "Wow!"
>
> But another student said, "He's just kidding."
>
> "Well, wait and see," said the writer. Beckoning for them to follow, the writer led them to a room with a display of a 15,000-year-old piece of carved reindeer antler.

During the tour, the playful metaphor of an invisible princess was used to spark discussion. Why would the magical princess have chosen specific pieces to put in her display cases or on her walls? What did she see in them?

Why had certain paintings been placed near one another? When the students reached the 20th-century exhibit, their discussion centered on how some paintings could be a depiction, not of anything a person can see, but of a feeling, something invisible inside. The writer explained that no one knows exactly what specific paintings "meant," only that these paintings allowed the invisible princess to express her different moods and feelings. That made each painting into a mystery, waiting to be figured out.

As the writing part of the tour began, each student received a clipboard with paper and a pencil. At each stop along the tour, the children drew and wrote, recording their own feelings and hunches, either directly in response to the art—or more indirectly by writing about the invisible princess and the art she had chosen to surround herself with. The princess also became a subject of discussion as the writer asked a few questions: What did the students think she might look like? Was it necessary for a princess to have flowing dresses and long blond hair? What about a princess who lives in a hot place like Africa or on one of the South Pacific islands? What would they expect a daughter of the emperor of Japan to be wearing? Might the princess be related to the Native Americans who lived in the area long ago? Or might she have traveled north from Mexico?

Because the students on these tours came from diverse neighborhoods, one or more children in several groups did not understand English or wrote only in Spanish. At times bilingual children helped, but they benefited from the tour's writer giving them encouragement for having publicly taken on that responsibility. A writer speaking to a dozen children from a neighborhood of mostly Latino residents began her tour by dealing with the basics: "How many of you speak Spanish? Who can translate what I'm saying for Luis?" As the tour progressed, the writer in residence talked about how many people from other countries visited the museum each year and how when Americans travel abroad art museums are favorite stops.

Using Art as a Stimulus

The overall goal of the Writing in the Museum project was twofold: (1) to sharpen students' artistic perceptions and (2) help students translate their visual observations into language that was meaningful to them. The writers in residence designed the museum tour to complement their regular work in the schools in support of the literacy curriculum. Children began writing poems and stories at the museum, then worked on them further in their classrooms. Asked about the benefits of the museum program, the writers cited three primary objectives: Students learned to observe closely; abstract concepts were made concrete and understandable by students in elementary school; the students experienced what it means to be an artist and a writer.

Observing. One teaching artist recalled her experience in guiding the students as follows: "I would have them look, then describe the painting to me without looking at it again. Usually they couldn't tell me much, so I'd tell them they could take another look." She remembered one particular art encounter as being especially meaningful, "This time they *really* looked at the painting deeply and could list off one thing after another. It got them ready for the sort of active looking they needed to do in the museum."

Another writer in residence commented, "Usually, I start by helping them to see what is familiar within what at first seems exotic and foreign, to build a bridge that gives them a relationship to the art."

A third writer added, "I like to get students to notice differences in what they perceive, like in the journal entry where I had them all look at a painting, write about it, then read their entry to us."

Abstraction Made Concrete. One writer in residence explained her process:

"Often I read poems that express ideas related to the paintings, to try to get students to see the painting as a visual poem. Then students write poetry, responding to another image."

She elaborated further: "I talk to students about the decisions the museum made to hang works in certain places—the juxtaposition of images—so that looking at one sparks new thoughts about the other."

Being an Artist. Yet another writer in residence explained the work routines and ethos of the program:

We treat their writing notebooks as art, an emblem of their experience, the thing they will keep, and we fill the notebook in all sorts of interesting ways."

She added, "Every page is different, with stories, poems, lots of kinds of drawing, answers to questions. Sometimes I have them break up the page, with different pieces that fit together like a stained glass window.

She gave another clue about her technique for eliciting expressive writing: "I have students view groups of paintings in a certain sequence. Then I ask students to create a story that bridges the gaps between the groups of paintings."

Another writer in residence encouraged his group of 4th-graders to build an imaginative connection to the art. He asked them to sit down opposite an exhibit of Native American masks and consider what it meant years ago for individuals in the mask maker's community to put on a mask like this. Here is the conversation he had with his group:

"Have you ever worn a mask?" he asked.
"Yeah," the children replied in almost a chorus.
"What's different when you put a mask on?" the writer continued.
"You don't look the same," one child offered.
"Is it good to look different?"
"Yeah," a child responded.
"What else do you notice?" he asked.
"You only smell the mask," a student chimed in.
"Do people treat you differently?"
"They might run away," a student called out.
"Why would they run away?" the writer probed.
"They might be scared," a child answered.

Having warmed up his crowd, the writer explained, "These masks all stand for wild animals." And he further elaborated about the masks: "They represent different clans."

The museum guard who accompanied the group stepped forward to explain further: "That raven mask is a rain hat. There's wire that makes the wings flap up and down. It's used in a ceremony to make the rain come."

Then the writing artist set his coterie of developing writers on a mission with the following remarks: "So, this mask was supposed to have certain powers. What powers would you guess the other masks might have? Let's all write the beginning of a story about what happened when some people decided to put on these masks."

Returning to Classroom After the Museum Visit

The way that the museum experience was built into the in-school writing program is exemplified by the following lesson, which took place in an upper elementary class for English learners a week after their museum visit. The classroom teacher was an animated woman who deftly used her voice, gestures, and facial expression to invite her 30 students to willingly participate in creative activities, despite any shyness engendered by their lingering struggles with English. She had arranged for the typing of her students' handwritten stories and riddles, conceived during their museum tour the week before. The teacher asked for volunteers to read them aloud. Two of the student pieces focused on trees in the park next to the museum, where the class had eaten lunch. The leaves were starting to turn to red and gold. Here are their compositions:

Riddle

It is yellow like the sun. It sounds like you are erasing your paper.
It feels like my fingernail.
It smells like fresh grass after it rains.
Answer: a yellow leaf

The Old Tree and the New Tree

One day an old tree got so dry that he just fell to the ground and broke. But, before he fell, he dropped some seeds to the ground. A new tree is growing and replacing the old one. This story repeats again and again and again.

The open format of the creative writing exercises enabled English learners to write in an expressive manner, showcasing their individual voices. This, in turn, enabled them to work at the cognitive level they were capable of, not just at the picture-book or basic-reader level of their English language skills. Students' bashful enthusiasm shined through as they read aloud and later discussed how they had arrived at their writing ideas. Magritte's surreal painting *Golconde* had captured the imagination of several students. Here are two students' compositions:

It seems like sad ghosts are coming out of the buildings. They look sad because they are wearing black clothes. It reminds me of a funeral . . . I think people in the building are praying for them. The buildings look sad too.

These people are in a hurry to get to work. It is a sad day. I can tell by the sad-looking purple. The building looks like an apartment complex. It may be that someone made a machine that makes people float in the sky. The people seem like they don't know what is happening. They think they are dreaming.

The use of informal conversation to stimulate students' reflection was a hallmark of the approach used by the writers in residence. Children experienced writing as an ongoing process, beginning with the original seed idea, with their process nurtured—through additional creative ideas and the feedback of others—so it grew into a finished work. Wong-Fillmore and Valadez (1985) found peer interaction important for enhancing oral second-language acquisition in students. In summing up the benefits she saw students gaining from the museum tour, a writer-in-residence commented as follows:

> When students are asked to write, all the ideas about correctness, about proper spelling and grammar, often intrude. Pointing out the "incorrect" yet powerful artistic expression of the modern artists can be one way of getting beyond this fixation on "correctness." Exploring all the varied ways that artists can express themselves is why I think children find the museum experience so powerful.

Children who took part in the museum writing tour experienced art in a personal way and learned how to transform their experience into writing. The use of art to trigger literary creativity ended up being funneled into the classroom. Although a week earlier these students had no idea what surrealism or abstract impressionism meant, they participated in animated group discussions about their personal responses. In this way, both the students' writing and their oral communication skills were enhanced. The museum tour exposed the students to a more sophisticated level of academic language than they had previously encountered in the classroom, for their teachers had tended to use vocabulary that most students would understand. Many students, who had been intrigued by the museum's surrealist paintings, enthusiastically used their new words in classroom discussions about the meaning of art.

At the end of the school year, a public reading of the children's poetry was given at the museum. Many of the parents who came to hear their children read their poems at first seemed bemused by the attention the children are receiving for their writing talent: The parents stared somewhat unbelieving at the people videotaping the reading for public television. Then they began to smile. They took in their surroundings, settled back, and enjoyed the presentation. Most had never been to a literary reading before or even heard of such an event. Yet there were their children. They listened and began to feel the power of this ancient ritual, whereby the person performing the reading was the one who had written the poem or story. After each child read her or his poem, the respective parents stood up and applauded. The students came to see their emerging writing skills as worthwhile, in part because of changes in their parents' views of their children's academic potential.

USING MEMORIES FOR INSPIRATION WITHIN CLASSROOMS

Using visual art to prompt student writing is an effective way to generate fresh new insights. Even so, the ongoing challenge of helping students uncover the stories that lie buried within their memories requires varied approaches. A teacher might find inspiration in unique cultural practices, such as the storytelling traditions of Native American tribes. People relying on an oral culture without a written language invent other ways to remember things, relying on pictures, poetry, rhythm, rhyme, and ritual to preserve their knowledge of the past (Egan, 1997).

The Lakota (like other Native American tribes on the Great Plains) maintained historical calendars made up of "winter counts." Each year, the tribal historian depicted a significant event on a buffalo or deer skin, organizing the pictographs in chronological order. This served as a mnemonic device, spurring people's memories and providing an outline for the group's oral historian to follow whenever recounting the tribal history (Smithsonian Institution, 2013). The story behind each pictograph was passed on orally from one generation to the next, much as stories are informally passed on during family gatherings.

Winter counts became a popular theme among Houston writers in residence who worked in the classrooms. After learning about the idea of winter counts, the writers asked students to think of a memorable event from the past year (or several years); these might range from the birth of a sibling, to moving to a new home or discovery of a new talent. After creating a stick figure representation (or storyboard), each student wrote a narrative explaining his or her pictograph. Other students peer-reviewed the narrative before the author revised it and then shared his or her narrative with the rest of the class.

THE POETS OF EL SOL ACADEMY

El Sol Academy of Arts and Sciences, the first dual immersion elementary school in the city of Santa Ana, California, has developed a unique poetry program led by writer in residence Sue Cronmiller. In kindergarten classes, 90% of the instruction happens in Spanish and 10% is in English; in 1st grade, 80% of the instruction occurs in Spanish and 20% is in English. In 3rd-grade, students start the poetry program and 40% of their instruction is in English. The school designed the poetry curriculum to engage El Sol's 3rd-grade students in English language instruction in a distinctive way, by awakening their interest in using imaginative language:

> Modeled after university seminars in creative writing, poetry workshops at El Sol expose elementary students to poetic work of cultural and historical significance and carefully guide the inspiration, drafting, writing and revision of their own original poetry. University creative writing workshops employ constructivist teaching methods, in so far as the students are more actively involved than in a traditional classroom. (Cronmiller, 2007, p. 4)

Following the Iowa Workshop model popularized in the 1950s, in which small groups of students meet with an instructor to discuss one another's work and offer suggestions, students from the University of California–Irvine lead small-group discussions of the children's poetry at the El Sol Academy. Before such discussions can begin, the children must be inspired to write. Each lesson starts with a whole-class activity led by an experienced writer in residence. In keeping with the literacy curriculum, students not only learn to write imaginative verse but also gain an appreciation for the function of nouns, adjectives, and adverbs while exploring new vocabulary words.

The first lesson typically begins with a playful exercise (Cronmiller, 2007). On the far-right side of the whiteboard, the class helped make a list of things, which the students learned can be called "nouns." The writer in residence encouraged the students to think of very specific nouns. So, if a child suggested *dog*, the writer asked what breed the dog is or its size. In the process of coming up with words, some children suggested words that are not nouns. That provided the writer the chance for a quick review of what makes a word a "noun." Although the tone remained playful, this quick review also led the students to think more deeply about grammatical concepts to which they have heretofore given little thought.

After the class came up with a list of five or six nouns, the writer-in-residence began a new word list in the center of the board, calling these descriptive words "adjectives." The writer encouraged children to contribute any adjectives that they found interesting, words like *mysterious*, *sensational*, or *naughty*. Coming up with words that qualified as adjectives was challenging, requiring several discussions about the difference between nouns and words that describe them. But because the writer made sure no one felt embarrassed, students eagerly participated in the process, gaining a firmer grasp of English grammar. When five or six adjectives were listed, there was another shift.

Then the writer in residence moved to the left side of the board and asked the children to choose an emotion. (A very good word for teachers to select is *love*, one of the most co-opted words in the English language, love is often described in sentimental clichés or symbols like hearts and flowers.) The writer in residence listed *love* five or six times, adding articles and verbs to make simple, one-sentence similes. The results of the exercise looked like the list on the following page.

First, the writer and the students discussed the simile and its use of comparisons based on the words *like* or *as*. Then they discussed the merit of each statement: Is love mysterious? In what way? Can a moth be mysterious? How? What do the children know about a moth that seems similar to what they know about love? Does this simile "feel" true? Does it have a sense of being true, without being literally true? Which of the similes seems to be least true or interesting?

Emotion	Adjective	Noun
Love (is as)	mysterious (as a)	moth
Love (is as)	naughty (as a)	rhinoceros
Love (is as)	perplexing (as a)	wishbone
Love (is as)	electric (as a)	Chihuahua
Love (is as)	magnificent (as a)	sand castle

The instructor who leads this activity must be willing to trust the process —and be inspired by the words that students contribute. Writing poetry is itself a poetic process in which logic and connection frequently come together in unexpected ways. The instructors often introduce this lesson in autumn just as members of the community are preparing for Halloween. One class produced the simile: "Love is as mysterious as bones." That metaphor inspired a conversation about love's role in the creation of life and its power in transcending death. At the end of the lesson, a student looked up in astonishment and commented, "Wow! I didn't know poetry could do that!"

Once students have seen how the simile exercise works, they usually are happy to independently create their own lists of favorite things and interesting adjectives and then pair the words in original one-sentence similes. So that helpful feedback is readily available, children at El Sol work in small groups and receive coaching from university students. But parent volunteers could be just as helpful. Here are two examples from a typical first lesson:

Love is as scary as a history project.

Sadness is as circular as an egg.

These examples demonstrate the young student writers' inspired interplay with the larger world. By activating the children's insight and observational skills, the exercise permits them to synthesize interesting facts and concepts and verbalize—on their own terms—their mastery of such ideas. In other writing lessons, students discuss the function of similes and are encouraged to create similes with concrete, sensory details; this helps them create fresh, imaginative figurative language (Cronmiller, 2007).

Such lessons acknowledge children's ability to appreciate, discuss, and grapple with complex human questions. As a result, the students take great pains to express themselves, using advanced vocabulary to explore and reconcile complicated individual and philosophical conflicts. By the end of 1 year, a student was able to write the following poem:

Love is as dark as a dragonfly.
Love looks like my grandma, chasing chickens on her farm in Mexico.
I see her long, red dress running around the farm.
Shiny sun, blue sky, green grass, white horses, brown cows, yellow chickens,
White sheep, orange ducks, all around my grandma, her shiny hair in the wind.
I remember her brown eyes, her wrinkled face.
I remember her dry, kind, hardworking hands.

El Sol allows students who are more comfortable writing in Spanish to initially do so, as long as they translate their finished poem into English. This supports students' ability to work in both languages. In another lesson, students create a simile for each of the five senses. They are asked to keep a list of interesting words they hear as the instructor reads poems. In later lessons, the instructor encourages students to use words from their list (or "word bank") in their poems. Simple prompts such as "Having a friend is like …" support using words in interesting ways.

All students' work is collected and kept in the students' folders, so that they can revisit their pieces to revise and rewrite. Students in 4th or 5th grade often turn to their folders to look for ideas. Their focus shifts from "consuming" the creative products of others to exploring their own perceptions and experiences in two different languages and cultures. Here is one example:

El caballo verde con 300 rosas moradas
En su espalda corriendo en las montanas
retumblando entre la guerra.

The green horse has 300 purple roses
on his back, running in the mountains
thundering into war.

Possibilities to Consider

- Have you ever toyed with the idea of introducing more poetry into your classroom but worried that children might find it too abstract to be interesting?
- Are lessons on nouns, adjectives, and the meaning of words among the least satisfying aspects of your literacy curriculum?
- Would you like to see students take joy in expressing themselves creatively, using advanced vocabulary to describe experiences they had not verbalized before?

WRITING STORIES FROM PERSONAL EXPERIENCE

Writers in residence frequently mention their struggles in steering students to look beyond canned images and retelling movie or TV plots, which they have passively absorbed from the media. One experienced writer-in-residence shared the following:

> Creating an imaginary world, or an imaginary city, helps the children go beyond both their immediate surroundings and the media images they are familiar with. Creative dramatics activates the same process; for a moment they really believe it and enjoy it. They really experience it. Then I tell them to be careful not to lose their concentration as they go to their desks and begin to write.

Another writer in residence, inspired by a strong interest in the film industry, devised an effective method for building on students' familiarity with movies and television. The writer led the following lesson near the end of a multiweek project, first asking students to recall an experience that had changed the way they saw some aspect of the world:

> Close your eyes and imagine a time when there was a change in the way you saw the world. It could be a small change, or a larger change. That doesn't matter. Just try to vividly recall an experience that changed the way you perceived people or events (or perhaps the choices open to you). Quickly describe what happened. For now, it is important to just get as much as you can down on paper.

That moment of change became the seed of a story. To make the revising process easier, each student later typed and saved their story on a computer. The next week, during the writing workshop, students were asked to think back and describe how they had first met the people in their story (or discuss their ongoing relationship with them). Students then revised the original plot of the story to include the evolution of one or more of these relationships. This revision provided the plot summary for the story. At this point, the instructor invited the students to change the names of places and characters, so as to encourage creativity and allow students to draw upon other experiences.

Before the next workshop took place, the students printed a copy of their plot summary. At the next workshop, the writer in residence asked students to envision a film crew arriving to dramatize their story. Scriptwriters would help with the dialogue. The writer told the students the following:

Imagine that the scriptwriter has asked you to jot down any dialogue that you can recall from your original experience on a separate piece of paper. Number the bits of dialogue. Then look over your plot summary and insert the numbers for the bits of dialogue where they fit. If you can't remember exactly what people said, you can reconstruct chunks of dialogue that seem to fit the characters.

Over the next week, students studied conversations depicted in stories they had recently read. Following these examples, they added the chunks of dialogue to their digital plot summaries.

The third workshop focused on set design. Students viewed video clips where the setting shown added significantly to the story's impact. Then the instructor guided the students to fill in the backdrop for their stories through these questions:

Where were the characters when the events in your story took place? Describe what the buildings, landscape, and onlookers looked like. What did the setting smell like? Put lots of immediate, sensory information into your description, so that readers can envision what it felt like and sounded like to be there.

Once the students wrote vivid descriptions, they inserted these details in the story where they best fit. Their goal was to help the future readers of their story be able to envision how the setting might have influenced the action.

In the following writing workshop, students were asked to examine their story from a film director's point of view. The director's job was to decide how the characters should move, speak, and gesture. Closing their eyes, the students pictured each person in the story, one by one, by asking themselves these questions: What do they look like? How old are they? How do they dress? What kind of posture does the character have? Do they have favorite phrases that they like to use? The students inserted these details into the text in order to bring the characters to life.

Finally, a costume designer provided students with detailed help in deciding what their characters would wear. This time, the approach was different. Students were not asked to describe what they—or their friends— wore at the time of the incident they were writing about. Instead of just describing the jeans or shirt someone may have worn at the time, students were urged to visualize clothes that told the reader more about a character. The writer guided the class with prompts like this:

Who wears the clothes? (The characters.)

So, we need to know about the personality of the character. Clothes show how a person wants to be seen by other people—or if they don't think about it. Choose a place where a key character first appears. Write a quick a physical description. Go ahead. I'll walk around. Just raise your hand if you'd like some help.

The writer then turned to one boy and commented about one of his characters, "Reddish hair? Good. What would someone who caught sight of him with the skateboard just then notice?"

And to a girl, "Yes, fantastic! I like the way you've used the smell of the hay and the horses. Smell is a really powerful sense that draws a lot of memories."

At the end of the project, when student volunteers read their stories to the class, the students' rapt attention attested to the meaningfulness of this opportunity to view the world through the eyes of their peers. Writing stories about their own experiences also invited students to contemplate how their own decisions may have shaped their experiences. Through writing some students learned to think more deeply about their experiences and imagine new possibilities. But to help students gain the full academic advantages of such a program, it is important to look more deeply at writing.

SKILLS-BASED GAINS IN STUDENT WRITING ABILITIES

The first section of this chapter explores how visual art can inspire students to produce written narratives. Subsequent sections examine how students can be assisted in creating poems and stories that are based on images and incidents taken from their lives. Stories occupy a unique position as a time-honored art form and a powerful tool for teaching. Eisner (2002) pointed out that thoughts can be difficult to hold onto if not stabilized by inscribing them on lasting materials. Both writing and the arts serve as vehicles for such preservation to occur. Even before the invention of writing, stories enriched by rhythm, rhyme, and powerful imagery served to preserve the history of tribal groups (Egan, 1997). This gives stories a unique status as both a powerful art form and a source of literary tradition.

Stories help people make sense of the world in two different ways. First, their familiarity with stories told by others assists individuals in deriving meaning from the input of their senses, which is often ambiguous and requires interpretation. The meaning that people assign to the sensory signals they receive confers significance on their experiences (Eisner, 2002), as do their actions. For young children, a remembered experience may be simple: The child says, "Cookie?" and his or her mother provides a cookie. Yet the significance for the child may be profound, demonstrating the usefulness of language (as opposed to crying or pointing) in achieving a specific goal. As the child grows older, the chain of cause and effect becomes more complex. Yet, building narratives around personal actions and associated sensory input remains critical to humans' making their experiences meaningful and memorable.

Second, stories provide a way of communicating personal experiences to others. Not only can people share their own stories, but the human capacity for imagination allows them to step into the shoes of others and experience indirectly what they have not directly experienced. This enables people to visualize situations they may eventually have to cope with (Eisner, 2002), providing the opportunity for mental rehearsal. Individuals can play out the consequences of various actions in their imagination and avoid taking the risks inherent in exploring those alternatives in real life.

Writing can confer yet another gift: the ability to preserve one's ideas, then build on them later. Once students become fluent readers, they are able to revisit a concept—or a story—with fresh eyes. That way, they can more carefully inspect, revise, and extend it. Or some individuals may recognize weaknesses they did not see before. These writers can then explore the areas of uncertainty, discarding notions that do not stand up to scrutiny, while building on those that do. For fluent readers and writers, this is a familiar process. In a moment of heightened insight, they quickly jot down a new idea. A few days later, they might take another look—and find the draft of the idea is much rougher than they initially realized. The original intuition is still recognizable, but considerable revision is needed.

This ability to re-engage with a narrative begun earlier becomes a pivotal academic skill for students in middle school and the grades beyond that. Even adults feel a sense of punctured pride when they return to a draft of a paper they earlier felt quite happy about, only to wince at how far the words on the page fall short of the message they had in mind while penning them: The sentences simply do not reflect the inspiration felt while writing. Like painters who envision a glorious sunset only to find—when brush touches canvas—that the colors look muddy and dull, writers struggle with the chasm between inspiration and implementation. Young students feel the same ways, so revising remains a skill that many of them resist learning. But the successful modification of a story so that it becomes a narrative they are truly proud of can convince students that revision is worthwhile.

One key to success is to help students generate a clear mental picture of their finished story. This makes it easier for them to generate drafts that come closer and closer to their goal. The designers of the short story project in the previous section had this in mind. Using a moment in their own life as the climax allows students to generate a clear mental picture of the story plot. Their emotional investment in exploring this moment of personal change strengthens their motivation. Of course, not all students will have the same level of focus. But for those willing to go through the process of revising and adding detail to their story—so that they can truly capture that "aha!" moment—the result is a deeper understanding of the nature of the writing process.

Examples of lesson plans, videos, resources, and teaching materials mentioned in this chapter may be accessed at the following website: http://sites.uci.edu/educ104donline/

CHAPTER 7

Expression Through Informational and Persuasive Writing

On a bright spring afternoon, parent volunteers brought bunches of flowers to school. The adults invited each 3rd-grader to choose a flower. As the children selected a blossom, a short video with flower paintings by Georgia O'Keeffe played in the background. When they returned to their seats, the teacher led the children through a close inspection of their flowers. Holding the blossom in one hand, the children used their other hand to draw the flower in the air with one finger. Next, the students laid their flowers beside some watercolor paper. Using a finger, they drew the outline of the blossom on the paper, large enough so that the petals reached each side of the paper. Finally, the children picked up a crayon and drew a sketch of their flower, going back over the outline to deepen the color on the paper. This created a "wax resist" pattern that gave structure to their painting.

The day before, with the help of their teacher, the class had explored their associations with color. This helped them decide which color they wanted the outline for their flower to be. The following metaphors about the three primary colors remained on the board:

Yellow warms the fields as sunflowers wake to a new dawn.
Blue, the elusive color of sky and sea, remains mysteriously untouchable.
Red exudes the power of a scarlet rose, a beating heart, a hopeful glance.

Once they finished retracing their outline, children used watercolors to fill it in, trying to reproduce the variations in hue in their flower. Many of their paintings were striking.

After the painting workshop, the students wrote in their art journals, reflecting on why they chose their flower, the color crayon they selected for their outline, and other design decisions. Previously, the class had discussed primary and secondary colors. Remembering the discussion, many students had chosen a shade that was a complementary color to their flower for the wax resist: So, the colors in their paintings seemed to "pop." The next week, their pictures were displayed on the bulletin board. Students were asked to pick a painting by a peer and write a short paragraph, reflecting on what they liked about the image.

Most weeks, the students drew (or pasted) their Friday afternoon art assignments right into their art journals, titled "My Third Grade Journey." The previous week the assignment had been a three-line haiku, written and illustrated with colored pencils.

The literacy objective of these assignments was to encourage students to produce clear, coherent written reflections, with text organized in a manner appropriate to the task and audience. The students followed each art workshop by writing a reflection, focused on the image created or the thought process that had inspired the image. In autumn, students collected colorful fallen leaves, carefully cutting them in half, with the stem preserved intact. The students glued their half of a leaf to drawing paper. Children closely inspected the leaf and wrote a description in their journal, which noted the shape of the edges and degree of symmetry, counting the points or curves, and discerning the colors. With colored pencils, they drew the missing side of the leaf, starting at the stem and moving outward until they reproduced the other half. Then they wrote a brief paragraph explaining why trees shed their leaves in autumn.

Down the hall, 4th-graders started a 2-week Halloween project, which included choosing a tale from *Aesop's Fables*[10] for their table group to act out after creating masks for the characters and a script. In their journals, students recorded their script and compared the portrayal of cartoon characters like Bugs Bunny and Wile E. Coyote with how ancient fables used animals to convey human characteristics. While working on their scripts, the students discussed—then wrote about—the range of behaviors available to a real rabbit or coyote as compared with what humans can do. Each group addressed the prompt "What advice may Aesop have been trying to give us?"

The integrated nature of the art journal lessons enabled teachers to utilize time that would otherwise have been characterized by student restlessness to introduce art projects. Because students tended to become restless on Friday afternoons, the hands-on aspect of arts-based assignments deterred off-task behavior. Moreover, the scope of the art journal lessons was flexible enough that the teachers could incorporate into them a review (from another perspective) of concepts that students had struggled with earlier in the week. The affective element introduced by the arts, along with the experience of sharing in creative endeavors, built a sense of community in the classroom. Art journal lessons began with the teacher sharing examples of good writing from the week before, thereby boosting students' motivation. Yet, although journal writing helped students build vocabulary and fluency, it did not include direct writing instruction.

---

10. Aesop's Fables: http://www.taleswithmorals.com/

TEACHING WRITING THROUGH THE ARTS

Informational writing is essentially a form of problem solving. Determining what the reader needs to know, then deciding what kind of explanation to provide, makes writing an intricate undertaking (Bruer, 1993; Hayes & Flower, 2016). The challenge is rooted in the fact that writing is a skill whose "kaleidoscopic" nature requires the orchestration of many component skills (Dyson & Freedman, 2003). Nonetheless, writing is a component of the English language arts curriculum that is critical to preparing 4th- and 5th-graders for success in middle school. For 5th-graders, the expectation is that, by the end of the year, they should be able to "write informative/explanatory texts to examine a topic and convey ideas and information clearly" (CCSS.ELA-LITERACY.W.5.2).

If a writer conveys an insight effectively, readers can grasp what the author is saying and become interested enough to follow the explanation to its conclusion. Writers must also be able to address the needs of readers with diverse interests, ability levels, and backgrounds. To make a discussion of concepts come alive, a writer has to provide readers with information on a variety of conceptual and linguistic levels. No ready-made formula exists.

Getting Started

When sitting down to write, students in upper elementary school tend to find staring at a blank paper daunting. They are unaccustomed to generating words without an audience inviting them to go on. In conversation, people provide one another with cues, asking questions for clarification, providing memory aids, and helping the others involved stay on topic. In written composition, these conversational supports are missing. This makes writing a harder and fundamentally different challenge from conversation. Even more difficult is the task of activating and searching the appropriate memory stores to recall relevant information in the absence of conversational prompts (Bereiter & Scardamalia, 1987). This explains why texts by novices are usually "writer based," meaning the text is structured according to the writer's experience, as opposed to what readers need to know to make sense of the information conveyed.

Using cues from their assignment, novice writers search their long-term memory for information about a topic; then they write down what they retrieve. In contrast to what happens during a conversation, when a partner conveys incomprehension, disbelief, or boredom and prompts a speaker's spontaneous self-evaluation, nothing signals the novice engaged in writing that readers may have trouble understanding what he or she has put down (Bereiter & Scardamalia, 1982). Fortunately, teachers can help students overcome such difficulties by embedding written assignments within a broader dialogue that includes oral and written components. This enables student writers to better judge which facts and explanations are needed if readers are to comprehend what they are trying to convey.

Creating a Classroom Dialogue

To initiate a broader dialogue, teachers may choose to assign 5th-graders a quick write. This requires every student to provide a brief, individual written response to a problem posed in the teacher's prompt. Each student must at least jot down a few initial thoughts. These ideas are then revisited during the following class discussion. Although the class might discuss the ideas of only two or three student volunteers, all students benefit from transporting their thinking from mind to paper and hearing how their teacher and peers respond to the ideas of the most confident writers. Later, the teacher can ask students to flesh out their initial ideas, using insights sparked by the class discussion. Of course, for students to benefit, they must be willing to invest energy and thought into carrying out the assigned tasks. The topic must be interesting enough to engage their attention. Students must also possess the knowledge to respond meaningfully.

Asking the class to write an opinion piece about a work of art can effectively spark interest and avoid a situation where students know too little about a topic to write anything meaningful. Furthermore, multiple options exist for interpreting a work of visual art. Students need only describe what they see, express their opinion about what it means, and cite evidence from the piece to justify their interpretation. Nor is age a barrier. Long before children master the skill of writing, they naturally connect thoughts, words, and images (Cassano, 2014). When teachers choose images for students to write about in class, they can look for:

- **Lots of details**: Simple images do not offer much to analyze.
- **Characters:** Images with people or animals will provide more to write about.
- **Colors:** Colors that convey a mood give students something to respond to.
- **Spatial relationships:** How do the background and foreground relate? (Cassano, 2014)

To start their students off with writing, teachers may wish to use a set of structured questions such as the ones below, which were inspired by Project MUSE, a program of the Harvard Graduate School of Education that explored art museums' potential to serve as integral forums for education. One goal of that project was to help students develop skills of observation that could serve them in science as well as in art. Educators consolidated the project's findings and resources, which centered on a generic game, into a document called *The MUSE BOOK and Guide* (Davis, 1996). Students saw a work of art and jotted down what they noticed about the image. Next, they responded to questions from an instructor. Finally, they were asked if they had noticed anything beyond what they had seen the first time they looked. Questions that teachers might ask include the following:

- What colors do you see? (Students may answer verbally or write in their journal.)
- What objects do you see in the picture?
- What is going on (happening) in the image?
- Does anything you have noticed in this work of art remind you of your own life?
- Does this image seem true to life? How real has the artist made things look?
- What ideas and/or emotions does this image seem to express?
- Do you have a sense of how the artist may have felt when he or she created the image?
- Does the title of this work of art make sense to you? What would you have called it?
- Thinking back, what have you learned by looking at this image in different ways?
- Do you like this work of art more or less than when you first saw it? Why?

Over time, a teacher can adapt this exercise into a relatively brief activity by projecting an intriguing image on the wall and asking students to write a paragraph interpreting what they see. The questions could be included on a poster kept nearby so students can refer to them. Students express their interpretation of what the image means and cite evidence from the image to justify their opinion. Students may keep writing journals, which the teacher collects and checks intermittently. Not only paintings or photographs, but also images related to science or social studies lessons could be used as writing prompts. The goal is for students to become more articulate writers, comfortable at expressing their ideas clearly in writing, using complete sentences and vocabulary.

RESPONDING TO LITERATURE

The way literature is studied in schools can make it difficult for students who are reading chapter books to respond with the same sense of excitement and interest that adults exhibit when they choose to read voluntarily on their own time (Smagorinsky, 2007). We live in an era when, outside of what's prepared for schools, the publication of books is moving away from offering monomodal, graphically uniform, dense pages of print without illustrations (Kress & van Leeuwen, 2001). Commercial publications are increasingly moving in the direction of multimodality, with color illustrations, sophisticated layout and typography. At home, when a student watches a movie, his or her engagement with the narrative is supported by images that show the action, sound effects that heighten the sense of realism, and background music that invites emotional response. In school, such supports are often missing, making it more difficult for students to make meaning out of dense pages of print and to gamely approach writing essays about them.

One way for a teacher to address this problem when assigning a book report or essay is to encourage students to use simple visual tools to record and organize their thoughts. When students write a compare-and-contrast essay, they would be well served by using a Venn diagram made up of overlapping circles. If a student author is comparing two characters in a story, what the characters have in common would be listed where the two circles overlap. Then the student can insert the words and phrases that uniquely describe the looks, personality, and behavior of Character A on the left side of the diagram, with the descriptors that uniquely describe Character B placed on the right side. Alternatively, if a student is writing about a Dr. Jekyll–Mr. Hyde type of character, the two sides of that character could be compared in the same way. In some books, two characters may seem in the beginning to have nothing in common, yet by the end they seem linked in important ways. If so, the student can compare the contrasting characteristics in the start of the essay with the commonalties saved for the discussion at the end. The report could even include a version of the Venn diagram as a visual aid for the reader.

Concept maps can be used in class for students to analyze more complex works, enabling then to consider more complicated ideas. Highlighting connections by using a concept map helps students see how individual ideas relate to a larger whole. Concepts and information are represented as boxes or circles, which are connected by labeled arrows in a downward-branching hierarchical structure. A concept map functions in much the same way as a traditional outline, but it requires students to do less advance planning in deciding where to slot specific concepts in the final structure. If students are planning to write a biographic report on a writer, they can begin by creating just a circle with the author's name at the top of the page. They can then use arrows to connect that author's circle to labeled circles connoting key elements of the paper, such as "Why I chose this person," "Why he or she is famous," "thought-provoking quotes," "important facts," "interesting anecdotes," and "references." As the students' research proceeds, more information will be linked to the appropriate circles.

The student expresses relationships between the concepts by labeling the arrows with words or phrases, such as "causes," "requires," or "contributes" (Novak & Cañas, 2006). The most inclusive and general concepts go at the top of the map and the more specific, less general concepts are arranged hierarchically below. Students can do this by using the following steps (outlined in a short video from the University of Guelph Library):[11]

- Identify the main topic (at the top center) and brainstorm everything you know about it.
- Organize this information into main points or elements in the narrative.
- Start creating a map, branching out from the main points to supporting details, etcetera.
- Look for more connections, using arrows and symbols to show relationships among ideas.
- Include informative details such as events, explanatory diagrams, and definitions.
- Analyze how concepts on the map fit together, checking for accuracy, logic, and detail.
- Make sure you can verbally describe connections among ideas; update the map as needed.

Using this process, students can create a nuanced concept map for a novel with a complex plot. This enables the students to better keep track of answers to this essential question: Who did what to whom and when?

Creating a Map of a Book

In contrast to a static graphic organizer, which tasks students with filling in the expected answer, a hand-drawn concept map lets students start with what they see as the key elements of a book and explore further. For example, Chapter 3 explores the first book in the Harry Potter series as a Cinderella tale. A concept map based on this perspective might include as the main elements these steps in Harry's journey: (1) living with the Dursleys as an unwanted orphan; (2) being rescued by Hagrid, the half-giant; (3) arriving at Hogwarts; (4) forming friendships with Ron and Hermione; (5) joining the Quidditch team; (6) saving the Philosopher's Stone (called the Sorcerer's Stone in U.S. editions) from Voldemort; and (7) celebrating at the graduation feast. Like Cinderella, Harry progresses from being treated like a household servant by his family to being accepted, loved, and cared

11. How to Create a Concept Map: https://www.youtube.com/watch?v=sZJj6DwCqSU

for by people of much higher social status, who are able to recognize his intrinsic worth. As students continue to read, they can find details on who did what to whom and when for the boxes of subsidiary plot points, which branch off from the main steps and chart Harry's evolution from persecuted orphan to Hogwarts school hero.

Of course, this is a somewhat intellectual way of looking at Harry's adventures. A student might prefer to identify with Harry and vicariously experience events from his perspective. A reader taking this stance may identify the main elements of the story as Harry's friends, his enemies, and Hogwarts (whose magical nature shapes the story). A concept map rooted in this perspective could visualize Harry's journey as shaped by the larger struggle between good and evil that is going on in his world. Hagrid is sent to rescue Harry by the benevolent headmaster Albus Dumbledore, who had earlier been a mentor to Harry's parents. Arriving at Hogwarts, Harry follows his parents' example in becoming a member of Gryffindor House. Like his father did, Harry develops an uneasy relationship with members of Slytherin House (to which Voldemort once belonged). A student building a concept map based on these elements might include branches to trace Harry's discovery of how earlier events—mirrored in the magical heritage embodied in Hogwarts school—had molded his destiny and influenced his choices.

Alternatively, students might choose to organize their concept map around characters and events in the plot, focusing on the adventures of Harry and his friends. A concept map organized in this manner might look at the options open to Harry and how he responds to them. This perspective does not examine the choices that Harry makes as if they were somehow destined or inevitable: At every step along the way, a variety of choices seems to be open to Harry, many of which would have taken him in a different direction. A concept map based on the first book could identify the pivotal points as those moments when Harry is faced with decisions such as (1) whether he should leave the Dursleys and go with Hagrid, (2) if he should become a member of Slytherin or Gryffindor, and (3) whether he ought to stand up to Draco Malfoy and retrieve Neville's Remembrall. Despite the influence of past events, Harry's choices appear to be opening a path to further growth.

If the long-term goal of a writing curriculum is to help students learn to weigh evidence and make reasoned decisions about which material to use in reaching conclusions, then any of the concept maps described above would be acceptable. The objective of writing assignments would not be to see if students can interpret plot points like academics traditionally have but instead to help students analyze a text so they can discern patterns and develop a coherent argument about the meaning of a passage they have examined. Although a concept map is only a tool for analysis, not a finished paper, concept mapping can play a key role in helping students explore a text and organize their thoughts prior to writing. It also enables teachers to quickly assess where more work will be needed before writing begins.

Helping Students Create a Concept Map

Each of the Harry Potter concept maps above focuses on a particular aspect of the narrative, which a student writer is trying to understand. But students can be distracted by unrelated aspects of the narrative. Therefore, teachers can help by asking students to construct concept maps that respond to a specific question. A bit of brainstorming can facilitate this, with students considering the following questions: What interests me most about the story? What issues am I curious about? What seems confusing and needs further explanation? By identifying elements of the narrative that they would like to explore further, students end up enhancing their motivation to dig a little deeper. When working with novice writers, teachers share a key resource in helping them construct a question that will assist them in focusing.

Unexpected connections between important ideas can still be found, however. Concept maps may include cross-links, showing relationships between ideas in different domains of the map. Such links often represent creative leaps on the part of the map's author. For example, on a concept map of the Harry Potter books, a cross-link might detail how the Hogwarts school is closely related to Harry Potter's present and Voldemort's past. Even though Headmaster Dumbledore has created a benevolent school environment, evil wizards have left their mark. There are reasons for Harry's wariness.

Unlike static templates, concept maps can be expanded when students' knowledge and understanding grows. Charting students' journeys of discovery, these maps assist them as they uncover new connections, even as they integrate new concepts with older ideas. Often, a concept map can stand on its own as a component of the completed paper. In creating a map, students externalize their understanding of a topic. Having represented their learning in tangible form, they find it easier to further investigate areas of uncertainty. The concept map also allows a teacher to efficiently check students' understanding, provide immediate feedback, nudge them to strive for a deeper grasp of concepts, or ask questions that help correct a misunderstanding.

But can a conceptual map itself be considered art? Clearly it is not figurative art, although students should feel free to include sketches in their maps. Yet, if used as tools for students to explore the relationships between various concepts, such maps can take on the character of abstract art. Just as an abstract painting portrays what the artist thinks and feels, a concept map depicts a student's explorations and discoveries; therefore, it reports on the private process of making meaning, with the results eventually made public in a written report or essay. But any concern about the final product—and how it will be graded—should not distract students from the meaning-making process of research.

Inserting the step of making a concept map into the longer process of writing a report or essay encourages students to focus first on achieving a degree of mastery of the topic, before focusing on how results will be reported (and will be graded or judged). By glancing at students' concept maps and asking questions, teachers can coach students as they explore, supporting them in extending their grasp of a topic. This approach encourages learning for learning's sake, boosting students' intrinsic motivation to try to understand things (O'Keefe, Ben-Eliyahu, & Linnenbrink-Garcia, 2013), while reducing their fear of failure.

Possibilities to Consider

- Do your students sometimes struggle to see how various elements of a literary work relate to the meaning of the work as a whole?
- Would you like to help students look more closely at a text and organize their thoughts before they start to write an essay or a report about it?
- Might it be helpful to have a way to efficiently check students' preparedness to write and give immediate feedback and nudge them toward a deeper grasp of concepts?

Moving Freely Between Images and Words

As was mentioned in Chapter 1, Parsons (1992) summarized the benefits of integrating the arts at school in helping students (1) learn to discuss what is hard to see and (2) find ways to see what is hard to say. Concept maps support this process by helping students organize their ideas and impressions, making it possible for them to put into words what had heretofore remained unclear. Also, concept maps provide students a way to represent, through symbols, insights they had not been able to verbalize. By facilitating the interaction of aesthetic and linguistic means of comprehension, concept maps integrate insights derived from language and the arts.

Initial development of the capacity to move freely between images and words often appears in children at an early age, when with little help they develop the ability to use illustrations in picture books to boost their comprehension of the plot. Kress and van Leeuwen (2006) presented a strong case that educators should treat multimodal learning as seriously as linguistic communication, arguing that students' free movement between images and words should be developed further, not cut off prematurely in favor of monomodal, word-based learning. Kress (2009) asserted "the world of meaning is multimodal" (p. 19) and suggested that learning occurs when meaning-making is paired with sign making. Research on multimodal learning has supported this, indicating that significant cognitive and social benefits result from such engaging and meaningful study (Greenfader, Brouillette, & Farkas, 2015; Moses, 2013).

Examples of lesson plans, videos, resources, and teaching materials mentioned in this chapter may be accessed at the following website: http://sites.uci.edu/educ104donline/

CHAPTER 8

Building Executive Function Skills with Arts Activities

By Christa Greenfader

While helping his teacher in the school's vegetable garden, 4-year-old Theodore suggested that they give "a little less water" to the onions as opposed to the other vegetables in the garden, saying he likes "onions only a little and if we give them just a little bit of water, then they won't grow too much." Indeed, much of how children experience the world involves their immediate goals and finding ways to achieve them. A 4-month-old learns how to solicit a smile from her parent; a toddler tries multiple ways to retrieve a ball that has rolled out of reach. As they near kindergarten age, children establish clearer ideas about what they want and how to accomplish those goals. Arts-focused activities can assist them in refining their executive function skills. Their goal-oriented processes become more and more sophisticated as children begin school; students must become adept at controlling certain thoughts and behaviors in order to earn their teacher's approval, understand the concepts they are learning, and play cooperatively with new friends. Further, as children's language and subsequent literacy skills improve, they can verbalize their goals and eventually write them, initially articulating them for themselves and reworking them as needed, and then communicating their intentions and desires with others. These skills are required not only for academic success but they play an instrumental role in supporting individuals' work and relationships throughout life.

WHAT IS EXECUTIVE FUNCTION?

What is it that enables these critical goal-oriented behaviors? Developmental researchers point to executive function, defined by Blythe Corbett and her colleagues as "an overarching term that refers to mental control processes that enable physical, cognitive, and emotional self-control and are necessary to maintain effective goal-directed behavior" (Corbett, Constantine,

Hendren, Rocke, & Ozonoff, 2009, p. 210). In fact, executive function appears to underlie many aspects of the five key dimensions that the National Education Goals Panel (Kagan, Moore, & Bredekamp, 1995) identified as essential for school readiness: They include (1) physical well-being and motor development, including the requisite gross and fine motor skills like sitting for extended periods of time and using pens and pencils; (2) social–emotional development so as to interact socially and interpret and express feelings, which allows for cooperation; (3) curiosity, enthusiasm, creativity, and persistence in order to be able to pay attention, follow directions, and stay on task; (4) language development in vocabulary, print knowledge, narrative abilities, and phonological awareness; and (5) cognition and general knowledge of shapes and spatial relations, problem- solving techniques, logic, representational thought, and social conventions. Although executive function is closely related to self-regulation (the ability to direct one's actions and thoughts), it is not simply a behavior. Rather, executive function involves sophisticated, intentional mental processes that enable such regulatory behavior; in other words, self-regulation is often a behavioral manifestation of one's EF processes.

Developmentalists have suggested that executive function includes three main components: inhibitory control, working memory, and cognitive flexibility (Diamond, 2013; Miyake et al., 2000). Adele Diamond (2013) defined inhibitory control or inhibition as a person's ability to control his/ her "attention, behavior, thoughts, and/or emotions to override a strong internal predisposition or external lure" (p. 137). Students who lack inhibitory control struggle to focus on the task at hand and can be disruptive by jumping out of place or talking out of turn; they may face academic challenges and have trouble navigating peer relations.

Working memory refers to a person's mental capacity to store and retrieve information and use it as needed (Baddeley & Hitch, 1994; Diamond, 2013); this affects a person's ability to draw connections between unrelated events and make decisions.

Cognitive flexibility—also called attentional flexibility, cognitive shifting, or attention shifting—involves a person's ability to focus on or give attention to certain things while ignoring distractions (McClelland, Cameron, Wanless, & Murray, 2007), as well shift perspectives or approaches to adapt to different demands (Diamond, 2013). Those who possess weak cognitive flexibility skills can also struggle with attending to the task at hand because they struggle with adapting or conforming to a new set of rules, or a change in routine or environment.

Beginning in infancy and continuing through adolescence, these three processes develop concurrently (Hughes, 2011), working in concert to enable young children to direct their attention and behavior toward achieving a specific goal. The development of these processes appears to peak as children are beginning elementary school (Yeager & Yeager, 2013). It is easy to imagine how such goal-oriented abilities assist children in the early grades, as they begin to need to focus on academic tasks, inhibit certain urges, tap into and draw connections from their knowledge base, adapt to new environments, and accommodate new information. Indeed, there is a large and growing body of research indicating the role that executive function plays throughout the school years; greater EF skills are associated with higher academic achievement (Blair & Razza, 2007) as well as better social–emotional competencies (Bierman, Nix, Greenberg, Blair, & Domitrovich, 2008).

What Contributes to Executive Function?

Any teacher will attest to the fact that there are distinct differences between children in their EF abilities. Indeed, some children (and adults, for that matter!) seem to have an easier time complying with classroom expectations, making connections between different subjects and ideas, and adjusting to change. Both biological markers and environmental factors play a part in a child's development of executive function.

Executive function can be altered by environmental factors and perhaps enhanced by specific programs and activities that target boosting it. Socioeconomic status also plays a role in executive function development; children from low-income families perform less well on such tasks, compared to their middle-class peers (Blair & Raver, 2015). Other contributors to a child's level of executive function skills include family factors such as parenting practices and home learning (Blair et al., 2011; McClelland et al., 2007), as well as exposure to stressful environments (Blair et al., 2011). Understanding these factors can enable teachers to help students build executive function skills and create classroom conditions and activities—like the ones below—that contribute to these abilities.

A child's language abilities are also related to and perhaps necessary for the development of executive function (Müller, Jacques, Brocki, & Zelazo, 2009). And the relationship between language development and executive function appears to be bidirectional: Both emerge during a baby's first year and develop rapidly in the early years; furthermore, they rely on each other. It is easy to envision how children's language skills can help facilitate their executive function abilities. As children develop receptive vocabulary, they can understand what an adult expects of them and why. (For example, they understand when their teacher explains that if they sit patiently, they will get a turn.) Likewise, as they develop expressive vocabulary, they can verbalize certain frustrations and use language to work through problems—initially to themselves and then with others. Vygotsky (1967) indicated that this "private speech" is playing an essential role in cognitive development; language enables children to work through the cognitive processes and strategies required to obtain a goal or solve a problem. Further, as a symbol system, language lets children understand such goal-oriented processes and imprints these thoughts and desires into their growing knowledge base—to be tapped by working memory when they encounter new information, scenarios, and problems.

Executive function likewise plays a role in language development. The child who can pay attention to the task at hand, inhibit other urges, and efficiently process information in working memory has an easier time learning how to read than one who struggles in these areas. Consider Chapter 3's instructional idea of teachers asking students to identify character archetypes and relationship phenomena and sentiments that may be found across cultures. While allowing students the opportunity to draw connections between various narratives from different cultures and time periods, this activity also requires and fosters EF processes. In order to make such connections, students may have to inhibit preconceived ideas about some cultures and their differences from others; they have to be flexible in their thinking and attention to specific similarities. Working memory plays a critical role in helping children tap into their knowledge base and synthesize information.

For this reason, many researchers and educators have suggested that promoting language development and executive function as related activities may be especially effective. Arts activities, because of their appeal for children—and for other reasons to be discussed below—might be especially appropriate for encouraging such development.

How Are Arts Activities Related to Executive Function?

In their meta-analysis of research studies about arts education's impact on cognitive outcomes, Lori Hetland and Ellen Winner (2004) indicated that research had not thus far been able to draw a definitive causal link between arts participation and academic outcomes, although there is strong evidence indicating the impact of drama's effect on verbal abilities and music education's impact on academic performance, spatial abilities, and phonological awareness, as well as general intelligence (Winner, Goldstein, & Vincent-Lancrin, 2013). Indeed, Hetland and Winner (2004) had suggested that researchers seeking to detect such a link could focus on "reasonable bridges," such as the potential relationship between arts and higher-order cognitive processes or dispositions related to behaviors.

Many educators already sense that various arts activities—especially performing arts disciplines, the focus of this chapter—might be related to cognitive abilities. In drama, a child seemingly relies on multiple executive function elements. While involved in pretend play, a child holds multiple roles and settings in working memory, using this information to act out different scenarios. Additionally, he or she exercises inhibitory control in resisting the urge to jump out of character or ignore the setting. Finally, he or she utilizes cognitive flexibility in adapting to the evolving plot and character development. Similarly, violinists spend countless hours in the practice room, resisting distraction, holding multiple aspects of the music (rhythm, pitch, dynamics) in their working memory—all while adding their own interpretations. Perhaps a violinist will then perform with different groups of musicians or play the same song at different tempos, adapting to varying circumstances, sometimes without previous discussion or practice. Likewise, ballet dancers must control their bodies while responding to changing beats and moods in the music, also adapting to different circumstances and resisting any urge to fall out of character. Visual artists must maintain focus as they transfer envisioned images to a featureless surface. Artists in all these areas will attest to the tremendous amount of attentional focus and monitoring needed—as well as the cognitive flexibility and working memory required—to steadily hone their skills.

EVIDENCE FROM RESEARCH

Although there is only a small body of research that investigated the relationships between arts participation on any scale (private lessons, group programs, classroom activities) and executive function, the majority of the work to date has evidenced a relationship between music participation and executive function development. Neuroimaging studies have indicated differences between the brains of musicians and nonmusicians; some of these differences are found in the inferior frontal gyrus—an area that may be active when a person exerts executive function and attentional control (Aron, Fletcher, Bullmore, Sahakian, & Robbins, 2003). Additionally, researchers have linked various types and levels of participation in music activities to increased cognitive abilities, including spatial temporal reasoning (Rauscher et al., 1997) and general intelligence (Schellenberg & Moreno, 2010; Winner, Goldstein, & Vincent-Lancrin, 2013).

In their work demonstrating that music lessons influenced the intelligence of children 9 to 12 years old, Degé, Kubicek, and Schwarzer (2011) suggested that enhanced executive function skills, specifically selective attention and inhibition, partially explained why children who took music lessons exhibited higher IQ scores than those who did not. Works by Bialystok, Moreno, and their colleagues (Bialystok & DePape, 2009; Moreno, 2009, Moreno et al., 2011) have explored the relationships between music, language, and EF; though certainly interrelated, musicians tend to exhibit strong executive function skills, which might also explain the benefits in terms of language skills. Moreno and his colleagues (2011) compared the verbal and executive function skills (specifically inhibitory control) of children 4 to 6 years old who were randomly assigned to participate in music or visual arts. After only 20 days of training, children in the music group exhibited higher executive function and verbal skills than their peers in the visual arts group. Although outside of the scope of their study, the authors speculated that executive function—in this case, a child's ability to pay attention—might be the link between music training and language skills.

Although the following topic is much less explored, research examining the impact of drama participation on EF also suggests a potential link. Schellenberg (2004) examined the IQ, academic, and social skills of 132 children 6 years of age who were randomly assigned to four different activities: piano lessons, voice lessons, drama, or nothing. Consistent with other research showing the connection between music and intelligence, he found that members of both music groups performed better on attention and processing-speed tasks than those in the other groups. The children in the drama group performed better on social or adaptive behaviors, however. This finding aligns with the current discussion on executive function as such social and adaptive behaviors are related to cognitive flexibility and inhibitory control. In a large-scale study with more than 1,000 4th- and 5th-graders, Elaine M. Walker and her colleagues (Walker, McFadden, Tabone, & Finkelstein, 2011) found that students who participated in drama-based activities during social studies and language arts classes outperformed a control group of their peers on a host of procognitive measures, including completing homework on time, completing it in a satisfactory manner, volunteering for extra credit, staying on task and being attentive in class. Although not a direct measurement of executive function, such procognitive skills are certainly related to executive function skills. Additionally, Walker and her colleagues' results showed that these students had better academic outcomes as well; the authors speculated that the reason behind this might be enhanced executive function abilities.

Yet, despite the promising suggestion that drama activities may boost executive function, in her study of 83 kindergartners, Heather Smith (2010) did not find any impact on executive function from the children's participation in a drama-based language intervention program. Smith's research examined an intervention based on a Wolf Trap Early Learning Program in Georgia that aimed to promote language skills through dramatic play. Despite sharing many components that were similar to a program that has been shown to be effective in improving EF competencies (Tools of the Mind, discussed below), there were no differences between the EF abilities of children who received and did not receive the lessons. Smith speculated that one of the reasons why she found no significant benefit might be the fact that the kindergartners had only 13 lessons. (In contrast, Tools of Mind integrates an entire curriculum into daily activities over the course of a school year.) After all, a key to the success of most interventions is the dosage (or the number of activities) and a consistent approach in their implementation.

Theoretically, a link between drama and executive function seems plausible. One rationale for this relationship is found in role theory (Frydman, 2016), which considers the many roles a person undertakes throughout the day. In other words, each person's day consists of acting out different roles—at work, at home, or while running errands—that task each person with conforming to the conventions, expectations, values, and even language, of varied roles, depending on circumstances. Therefore, someone's ability to just make it through the day taps into all three components of EF. Most people are likely to exercise a greater degree of inhibitory control at work than at home. Yet a person still must keep track of the different conventions to be used in different settings, monitor his or her own actions and the responses to those actions (working memory), and adjust accordingly (cognitive flexibility). Drama activities heavily feature role-play and sometimes changing roles; therefore, they provide ample opportunities to develop and exercise such EF skills.

Teachers can promote the understanding of taking on various roles and changes by having students act out a scene from a story or poem from their language arts curriculum or even a history lesson. With their assignment to different roles, students have the opportunity to engage with the material in a fun way and to tap higher-order cognitive processes in interpreting the characters. Furthermore, the teacher can then ask the students to switch roles, so the students must change their understanding and approach. Plus, the teacher can introduce a change to the plot—or ask the students to create a different scenario—before they again act out the scene. While such an activity is appropriate for the complex plot lines and events found in higher elementary school grades, it can also be used in kindergarten. The teacher might take a popular children's fairytale such as that of Jack and Jill and ask students to create an alternative scenario (Jack and Jill are not climbing a hill for a bucket of water but driving to a farm to pick oranges) or add an embellishment to it (the two must hurry to get a bucket of water to put out a fire).

A final step would be for the class to engage in a discussion of how the characters had to adapt to changing circumstances and how various ones responded differently based on their backgrounds and points of view. Such an activity simultaneously encourages sophisticated verbal interactions and executive function processing.

Another theoretical link between drama and EF might be explained by research that has illustrated the relationship between pretend play and theory of mind (Jenkins & Astington, 2000). Theory of mind, the ability to understand that different people can think different things, is often assessed by a false belief task. In one example of this, a child is (1) shown a box of crayons, (2) asked what is inside (before the box is opened), (3) shown that there are candles inside, and (4) questioned what his friend (who has not witnessed the exchange) will think is inside the box. A child who displays theory of mind will answer "crayons" based on the expectation that crayon boxes contain crayons. But a child without theory of mind cannot imagine that his friend will not possess the same insight that he has just gained. The more a child engages in pretend play—and the more elaborate it is—the more this activity is likely to improve theory of mind. This play could be connected to executive function abilities as researchers have shown they predict theory of mind (Carlson, Mandell, & Williams, 2004; Hughes, 2011). Perhaps pretend play affects executive function, which in turn affects theory of mind.

Jean Piaget (1962), a pioneer in the study of children's cognitive development, suggested that dramatic play and creative movement activities come naturally to young children and serve a crucial role in their construction of meaning. Although he believed development unfolded as a child matures through four discrete stages, Piaget also recognized the importance of the child's experiences in his or her development. Recent neurobiological work has illustrated executive function's role in aiding a child's progress through each stage, as well as the growth of executive function within each stage (Bolton & Hattie, 2017): Some of this is based on neurophysiological development but a child's engagement with his or her environment also plays a part. As a child engages in creative play and other related activities, he or she might be honing cognitive skills—such as executive function—that are necessary for constructing meaning and further development.

Lev Vygotsky (1967), a contemporary of Piaget and also a key theorist of child development, indicated the significant role of play, noting, "In play a child is always above his average age, above his daily behavior; in play it is as though he were a head taller than himself" (p. 16). Vygotsky continued, "As in the focus of a magnifying glass, play contains all developmental tendencies in a condensed form; in play it is as though the child were trying to jump above the level of his normal behavior." Thus, dramatic play promotes intentional behavior as it taps into the higher-order mental processes (or executive function) necessary for self-regulation (Bodrova & Leong, 2015).

Elaborating further about play, Vygotsky (1967) wrote the following:

Play continually creates demands on the child to act against immediate impulse, i.e., to act according to the line of greatest resistance. I want to run off at once—this is perfectly clear—but the rules of the game order me to wait. Why does the child not do what he wants, spontaneously and at once? Because to observe the rules of the play structure promises much greater pleasure from the game than the gratification of an immediate impulse." (p. 14)

As Vygotsky points out, engaging in play activities at school is both fun and motivating, as well as social and interactive. Not only do the children interact with the teacher, but play and related arts-based activities in the classroom also present unique and creative opportunities for students to engage with one another and learn through collaboration. Through their interactions with teachers and peers, children become more adept at managing their behaviors and responses and continue and extend their involvement with dramatic narrative.

What About the Arts Might Aid Executive Function?

Drawing upon a career of investigating the effectiveness of various types of EF interventions, Adele Diamond (2012) posited that, in addition to stretching a child's EF competencies, there are four key components through which a program could impact EF: (1) increasing joy, (2) building confidence and self-efficacy, (3) fostering feelings of belonging and social support, and (4) promoting physical health and fitness. Although Diamond's research (and others') has not yet investigated arts programs as EF interventions, she suggests it as an area for research. Certainly, arts activities embody many aspects of executive function and the four components she identified. As this chapter discusses, performing arts disciplines are primed to challenge executive function competencies. Engaging in such activities gives children the opportunity to practice their inhibitory control, stretch their working memory capacity, and learn to adapt to new environments and information. Additionally, arts activities are fun and engaging, collaborative and team building. They promote movement and activity and offer children the opportunity to work hard and then witness the fruits of this effort, so they can feel proud of their accomplishments.

Built into arts activities are various techniques that rely on and extend executive function skills. Researchers have identified the following components of arts activities as strengthening long-term memory: rehearsal (or repetition), elaboration (extending what is known, anchoring new concepts to something familiar), generation (using a prompt or cue to further extend a concept or the plot), enactment (physically acting out an idea), oral production (connecting meaning and language), putting effort after meaning (participating in something that is engaging and fun instead of only exerting effort to learn the task at hand; a fun way to learn), emotional arousal (invoking emotions that support and anchor understanding), and pictorial representation (using visual aids for comprehension and retention) (Rinne, Gregory, Yarmolinskaya, & Hardiman, 2011). It is imaginable that these techniques also assist in supporting EF development, especially working memory and cognitive flexibility.

Grounded cognition theory and multimodal research offer further insight. Research on grounded cognition theory (sometimes referred to as embodied cognition theory) has found that comprehension and retention are boosted when learning is connected to meaningful movement, gestures, or expression (Glenberg, 2010). Multimodal research has netted similar results, showing the benefit of utilizing different learning modes (e.g., language and movement) of learning (Kress, 2009). Work in these fields has been used to explain a way that various arts activities and lessons support learning and development (see Greenfader et al., 2015). Such research relates to this chapter's discussion because executive function processes are seemingly involved in children's ability to work in, navigate between, and monitor their performance in multiple modes. Furthermore, neurophysiological evidence has indicated executive function and embodied cognition activities share similar brain regions and functions (Koziol, Budding, & Chidekel, 2012).

One curriculum that researchers have found effective in boosting the executive function performance of preschoolers and kindergartners is the Tools of the Mind curriculum (Bodrova & Leong, 2007; Diamond, Barnett, Thomas, & Munro, 2007), which draws upon certain practices found in arts activities. Grounded in Vygotskian theory focusing on the role of self-regulation in learning and development, Tools of the Mind helps teachers boost children's self-regulation skills by facilitating increasingly complex dramatic play, among other things. The Tools of the Mind curriculum approaches dramatic play as an effective mechanism for the development of self-regulation; as William Barnett noted, "dramatic play leads to the internalization of rules and expectations and places demands and constraints on a child's behavior" (Barnett et al., 2008, p. 302). To participate in a make-believe situation, a child must adhere to a certain set of social rules governing his or her actions and responses. The play activities in Tools of the Mind enable children to follow their interests to guide their play activities, while being closely monitored by the teacher, who facilitates opportunities for social interaction and more sophisticated scenarios. (See Barnett et al., 2008, and Diamond et al., 2007, for a further description of Tools of the Mind.)

Implications for Practice

A key takeaway from this chapter is that participation in performing arts activities may very likely help students improve in their executive function skills. How might elementary grade teachers incorporate arts-based activities into their already-full curricula, with learners of all different abilities, experiences, and languages? For teachers looking to foster executive function development while creating educational environments suitable for all learners in highly differentiated classrooms, an excellent option is including engaging, arts-based activities that intrinsically invite the participation of children with varying skill sets and abilities.

The Tools of the Mind curriculum (Bodrova & Leong, 2007) offers some sample exercises for children in the primary grades: One activity is the "Freeze Game," which targets children's development of two skills that involve executive function: self-regulation and symbolic representation. In the "Freeze Game," the children and teacher dance to music. During the dancing, the teacher holds up a picture of a stick figure in a specific pose. When the music stops, the children model that particular pose. Perhaps the most obvious executive function skill that this teaches is inhibitory control; the students must inhibit their urge to start the pose while the music is playing and curb the urge to continue dancing once the music stops. And it requires the children to translate the stick figure representation into an actual body position and adapt to different poses as the game continues.

Other curricula present different variations of this activity. In a dance lesson of the Teaching Artist Project (TAP), an elementary arts and literacy professional development program (Greenfader et al., 2015), children imitate a certain animal or portray an emotion as music plays and then follow specific instructions for the pose they will adopt once the music stops. A version of this called "Musical Octopi" from the Resilient Families Program (RFP) calls for a resiliency intervention targeted at boosting the self-regulation skills of at-risk children who dance to "ocean" music (e.g., *Finding Nemo* soundtrack), moving around as if they were octopi. When the music stops, they must lie down on the floor, put their hands on their stomach, and breathe deeply. Not only are these activities fun and helpful to children as they begin to regulate their behaviors, but they can be very useful for teachers in establishing classroom management.

In addition to the "Musical Octopi" example above, the Resilient Families Program also offers a wide variety of arts-based activities uniquely designed for teachers to implement in classrooms or for parents to utilize at home. Although this program primarily focuses on children old enough to attend preschool, nearly all of the activities can be used or adapted for children in the early elementary grades as well. One of its activities, called

"Wiggle Like an Octopus," has children pretend to be octopi and wiggle certain body parts, without moving other body parts. (TAP dance lessons also include a similar activity as a warm-up.) Such activities help children practice inhibition, as they must only move one area at a time. Another Resilient Families Program activity enables children to work in pairs while they create their own "patty-cake" rhythms together, clapping each other's hands. Once they are confident with their rhythmic pattern, they chant or sing a poem on top of the steady rhythm.

An interesting dramatic play opportunity is modeled in the Tools of the Mind activity called "Play Plans." Directed by the students and support-ed by the teachers, this activity enables children to preplan their dramatic play. Children write or draw the role that they will play and what they will do in it. Teachers act as resources for the students as they create their play plans, perhaps answering questions and offering suggestions for plot enhancements. Once students have completed their play plans, they have the opportunity to perform their play and, in doing so, they are tasked with sticking to the script (inhibiting their urges to break character or deviate from the plot), as well as potentially going back and modifying the script (using flexibility skills by adapting to different scenarios). Such plans can be used with children of multiple ages and abilities, ranging in sophistica-tion. An additional strategy for teachers in higher elementary grades is in-cluding a debriefing or evaluation part of the activity, allowing students to reflect on why they made certain choices, what worked, and what did not. Then they can modify their script based upon such feedback. Such a strate-gy has been incorporated in the Teaching Artist Project and found to help elementary school students improve their oral language (Greenfader et al., 2015). This has promising implications for boosting such executive func-tion competencies as working memory and cognitive flexibility as well.

Some teachers like to use music or dance activities as opportunities to practice turn taking, an important regulatory skill that children need to enjoy positive social interactions and academic success. A teacher could simply state, "My turn," and then clap or tap a rhythm or model a dance movement or pose, then say, "Your turn," indicating the entire group of stu-dents should imitate the rhythm, movement, or pose. Teachers can modify this activity's complexity by dividing the class into smaller groups with specific names (e.g., "blue" or "red"), and then after saying, "mMy turn," call for "Blue's turn." Or they might have different groups of students respond, depending on whether the teacher claps or taps. Some teachers prefer to play recorded music with each verse featuring specific instruments (drums, triangles, maracas, or castanets) and have each group of students play their assigned instrument when they hear it. If time permits, the teacher may choose to have the student groups switch instruments one or two times, requiring them to adjust their listening and processing skills.

For younger children, visual arts activities like drawing or sculpting can be useful for helping children think about calming down. Similar to creating "Play Plans," teachers might ask the students to think about a familiar object and what it looks like. To create that drawing, they must then choose the colors and size that match what they imagined. An enhancement of this exercise would be to ask the children to identify colors to represent various emotions and then to draw a pyramid (or another shape) with different levels. The child would start coloring the bottom part in the hue associated with the most negative emotions (such as angry or sad) and then shade the top area in the color identified for the most positive emotions (like excited). These activities can promote inhibitory control and working memory as they necessitate children to color certain parts in specific colors and remember which one relates to a specific emotion and in what order.

Finally, consider Chapter 3's example of storyboarding and how it can also connect to EF. As students work through visually presenting a timeline of a story's plot, their cognitive processes help enable them to focus on the task at hand and draw connections between different events and characters. Just as they need such executive function abilities to successfully create their storyboards, this visual portrayal of story elements can foster a visual representation or ordering of their thoughts and interpretations. This potentially serves a role similar to "private speech," which can aid children in developing more sophisticated cognitive processes.

This last example illustrates that there are likely many classroom practices that might not be explicitly linked to executive function skills but certainly require them and likely foster their development. Certainly, there are numerous arts-based activities and enhancements not mentioned in the current discussion that may assist young learners in building executive function skills. Many of these activities include—or can include—a language component as well, providing opportunities for children to learn receptive or expressive vocabulary, better understand narrative structure and discourse, and practice recall.

As researchers continue to explore ways that teachers and parents can help children develop these skills so critical for future success, educators can sprinkle engaging arts-based strategies into the classroom curriculum and home routines. Just as most young children readily engage in such activities as playing, singing, dancing, and drawing, many teachers and parents (consciously or unconsciously) are already incorporating arts-based practices that might serve as the basis for some of the techniques discussed above. The next step is simply to boost the effectiveness of these efforts through more discerning implementation.

Examples of lesson plans, videos, and teaching materials mentioned in this chapter may be accessed at the following website: http://sites.uci.edu/educ104donline/

CHAPTER 9

Bringing the Arts Back to the Language Arts

The world of young children is in constant motion. Toddlers spend a large part of their day exploring and engaging with their environment. On a daily basis, they may

> [T]ake more than 9,000 steps and travel the distance of more than 29 football fields. They travel over nearly a dozen different indoor and outdoor surfaces varying in friction, rigidity and texture. They visit nearly every room in their homes and they engage in balance and locomotion in the context of varied activities. (Adolph & Berger, 2006)

Yet, in today's high-tech world, young children's freedom of movement is curtailed as soon as they leave home. Streets are full of fast-moving cars. Even in a parking lot, a child is safer sitting in a stroller than walking. Cities, towns, and suburbs have been shaped by economic forces that have left few safe places for children to roam freely. In an attempt to keep children occupied, adults offer them iPads and computer games. But growing children feel a need to be physically mobile, investigating their environment. When opportunities to move and explore are denied for too long, children's frustration and restlessness build.

When such active youngsters first enter school, they can become twitchy and agitated when expected to sit quietly all day, listening to adults or focusing on worksheets. Even when they reach the higher grades, students' attention wanders if school fails to offer them opportunities for active engagement. Key elements of a lesson may go unheard. The integration of arts activities within a lesson, bringing an active, engaging dimension to classroom routines, lets teachers keep the spirit of exploration alive. Young dancers expand their vocabulary and their knowledge of verbs and adverbs as they listen to their teacher call out movements, then perform them: skipping merrily, stretching quietly, or wiggling rapidly. Drama games provide an excellent way for children to enhance their oral language skills. Drawing and painting let children explore variations in shape and color. Learning the songs of other eras expands students' historical awareness.

Artistic endeavors have been linked to the wide-awake quality of awareness (Greene, 1977), stimulating active attention as opposed to passive involvement (Schutz, 1967). Active attention requires focusing with full awareness: Examples of this include listening to news that a person has been eagerly awaiting or engaging in a project that demands complete concentration. Often, active attention is aroused by the element of novelty or surprise. Passive attention is more diffuse; one example is the somnambulant state of mind a person might enter into while watching a required presentation of limited interest to the viewer. Even adults find their minds wandering when a meeting goes on too long. Children find it even more difficult to concentrate for long periods of time if no appealing, concrete activity is available to help them focus their attention.

CHOOSING ARTS-BASED ACTIVITIES THAT REINFORCE LEARNING

At the beginning of Chapter 2, a teaching artist invited a kindergarten class to actively participate as he told a story; the children provided sound effects, which helped them imagine trekking through swishy grass and gooey mud.[12] Multisensory engagement aids kindergartners in focusing on the teaching artist's words and remembering the new vocabulary words that are introduced. When 1st- and 2nd-graders dramatize stories, this sensory experience enables them to better understand the plot and characters' feelings, even if they do not initially comprehend all the words. By using their bodies and voices to dramatize characters' words and actions, children gain a sense of how interactions among characters shape the events in the story (Mages, 2006). The concrete nature of dramatization lets children mentally represent events and characters for themselves. If they merely listen to the story, the English language learners in the class would have trouble understanding what is going on.

An unintended consequence of the push for standards-based education has been a focus on the reproduction of existing knowledge, rather than on activities that require students to engage in complex thinking and personal expression (Eisner, 1993). Articulating shared learning goals in literacy, math, science, social studies, and the arts that are appropriate for almost all students is valuable both to educators and to community members. But strategies that are narrowly aimed at moving students forward—like directing an army to march toward fixed and uniform goals—might fail to engage children who are thirsty for more chances at individual exploration.

12. Video of lesson: https://sites.uci.edu/class/kindergarten/theater-kindergarten/kindergarten-the-ater-lesson-2/

Arts integration provides each child an opportunity to connect with the curriculum at her or his developmental level. The heightened level of attention that Greene (1977) referred to as "wide-awakeness" can be accessed by all members of a class in an environment that invites investigation and invention. Discussions using Visual Thinking Strategies (Robertson, 2006; Yenawine, 2013)—presenting students an intriguing image and asking them to speculate about what is going on in it—provide students opportunities to share their reasoning ("What makes you say that?") and hone their critical thinking skills. Active attention is the key. As John Dewey (1934) noted, "Mind is primarily a verb. It denotes all the ways in which we deal consciously and expressly with the situations in which we find ourselves" (pp. 274–275).

What makes arts integration a uniquely useful tool for K–5 teachers is how easily a wide range of abstract concepts can be made concrete, so that children can mentally represent and remember what they have learned. Visual art, drama, dance, and music activities enable children who are not fluent writers (and thus unable to take notes to later jog their memories) to create vivid mental images of experiences, which they can readily recall. Simultaneously, the affective aspect of the arts creates an enhanced sense of community in the classroom.

EXPLORING HUMAN RELATIONSHIPS THROUGH STORIES

Through nearly all the eras of human history, most of what children learned about the wider world came from the stories told by family, friends, and acquaintances. Telling stories about a day's happenings continues to be a key way of sharing experiences, building understanding, and fending off loneliness. Long before children can read or write, they are already learning from stories shared by family members and the ones others read to them. A child's listening to stories, whether across the family dinner table or on a parent's lap, creates a sense of closeness and shared understanding as the youngster vicariously experiences the narrated events.

Chapter 3 explores the development of children's understanding of narrative by investigating how the archetypal tale of Cinderella (beloved even by children just starting kindergarten) becomes riveting for older students when the story is transformed into a tale about a more contemporary orphan who is also forced into a servant role by his relatives (Rowling, 1997). Finally, we look at a real-life tale that follows a similar pattern: Dr. Adeline Yen Mah's (1999) autobiographical story, *Chinese Cinderella*. Such stories of unjust oppression and exultant reward have thousands of variants around the world. Their popularity is rooted in the fact that almost all children feel at one time or another unappreciated and misunderstood.

Dr. Mah's tale describes how deeply moved she was as a child after reading *A Little Princess* (Burnett, 1905), the story of a young girl who overcomes impoverished circumstances through perseverance.

In Harry Potter, children around the world have found a hero whose adventures both boys and girls can relate to. When we meet him as an 11-year-old boy, Harry focuses not on finding romantic love but on affection and camaraderie. Harry's journey has many similarities to the Cinderella tale. But while the original Cinderella tale depicts archetypal figures whose characteristics do not change, the Harry Potter books show his skills and sense of agency expand over time. Yet, until the final books, other characters (Harry's loyal wingman Ron; the smart, bossy Hermione; benevolent Headmaster Dumbledore) change little. In contrast, *Chinese Cinderella* shows how the choices of individual family members shape their personal evolution and the future opportunities open to them.

TEACHING ABSTRACT CONCEPTS TO CONCRETE THINKERS

The Common Core State Standards put increased emphasis on informational text, which creates a challenge for K–5 teachers: Many students have difficulty with the concise, precise academic language used in science and social studies texts. The sophisticated vocabulary used in the STEM fields is especially difficult for English language learners. Arts-based science activities, which children often perceive as play, invite students to use new technical vocabulary words as part of activities that clarify the meaning of the concepts represented by these terms. Drawing and creative moment provide children who are not yet abstract thinkers with concrete ways of envisioning phenomena that they cannot directly observe. This enables teachers to discuss concepts that would be difficult to describe if they were to use only words that all 8- or 9-year-olds know.

As we saw in Chapter 4, the creation of the Next Generation Science Standards (NGSS) was rooted in the assumption that progressively more sophisticated explanations should be provided as children's understanding grows. Teachers of K–5 students may wish to utilize arts-based metaphors that provide children with an initial grasp of concepts, then elaborate on the concepts in later lessons, as students become more comfortable with the academic language of science. Visualization is integral to scientific thinking. After all, scientists imagine new relationships and test ideas through visual representations. In keeping with this tradition, visual art lessons that focus on recording observations in science notebooks encourage students to look closely at natural objects, helping them improve their observation skills.

Social studies concepts are also abstract and they can be more difficult for educators to represent. But, as noted in Chapter 5, the songs of past eras can convey the perspective of people who lived through events described in a history unit. When the perceptions expressed in two songs differ, as is the case with "Yankee Doodle" and the "Library Song," students may enjoy discussing how the feelings expressed in each song influenced the attitudes of people who identified with those differing viewpoints. For example, the song "Yankee Doodle" was originally used by the British to make fun of American colonists. Later, the same song was adopted by the colonists to mock the British after the tide of the war began to turn in the colonists' favor. Students can experience the thrill of discovery in learning about the origins of a song they may have dismissed as ordinary and rather silly.

THE ACQUISITION OF NARRATIVE SKILLS

At a time when the stories of families and friends can too easily be drowned out by narratives streamed from the electronic devices all around them, students often have trouble telling their individual stories. When asked to write a story, children who spend hours watching television daily may assume that a story from their own life could not possibly be as interesting as a narrative in popular culture or their own version of such a narrative. Furthermore, when families watch television during mealtimes and parents do not make a practice of asking children about their day, children may get little practice in describing their experiences. Such students need support in developing their own voices. Storytelling can be a powerful tool for helping these students become confident enough to share their experiences.

Chapter 6 includes a strategy for using students' familiarity with movies and television to help them create and flesh out a narrative based on a memorable incident in their life. Happy moments work well. Students might describe a time when they accomplished a long-sought goal or when they worried about an issue that in the end turned out well. But students sometimes feel a need to get something off their chest by describing a troubling incident. If an event stands out in a student's memory, this signifies an emotional resonance; its climax can make a moving conclusion for a story. The first step for students is to put down on paper a description of the incident. Then, if possible, the description is transferred to a computer, so that the student can more easily expand the narrative. If a computer is not available, a student can draft new sections on separate pieces of paper to later add to the story. In step two, the student describes what led up to the climactic incident (perhaps describing the frustration that he or she felt in trying to reach their goal, followed by the events and circumstances that made success possible).

This is the point when students' familiarity with film and television becomes helpful. Students are asked to imagine that their story is going to be made into a film. Dialogue is needed. What conversations took place during—or leading up to—the pivotal moment? Rarely can the exact words be recalled, but dialogue expressing the mood and intent of those involved suffices. Taking on the role of the director, students ask themselves the following: What gestures do the characters make? What are their facial expressions and tone of voice? Students then take on the role of set designer, describing the setting and its impact on the action: Are there onlookers? What is the weather like? What time of day does the action take place? At the end of this activity, students create a first draft of an original story. They will also have begun to realize that their own experiences may be more interesting to others than they had originally thought.

MAKING CONNECTIONS AND REVEALING UNDERLYING STRUCTURE

The contribution of the arts to informational and persuasive writing tends to be more abstract. Nevertheless, students benefit from having a way to represent information that enables them to more effectively envision and utilize it. When people sketch a map to show a friend how to get somewhere or study a blueprint before remodeling their house, they may not think of the sketch or blueprint as art. Yet, this is where humans connect most directly with the primeval meaning of art as John Dewey (1934) described it in *Art as Experience*:

> A work of art elicits and accentuates this quality of being a whole and of belonging to the larger, all-inclusive, whole which is the universe . . . somehow, the work of art operates to deepen and to raise to great clarity that sense of an enveloping unidentified whole that accompanies every normal experience. (p. 195)

In sketching a map, a person shows how a friend's destination relates to a larger whole, within which roads will facilitate his or her travel. When individuals study the blueprint of their house, they are reminded that the physical structure they live in is a complex work of art, connected by hidden pipes and wires to a larger civilization that continuously supplies them with water, heat, and light. The blueprint acts as a map, enabling people to cut through walls without damaging these connections; as a work of art, it helps humans to see the larger meaning of the acts they are involved in. Dewey (1977) noted this when speaking to an audience of teachers:

> To feel the meaning of what one is doing and to rejoice in that meaning; to unite in one concurrent fact the unfolding of the inner life and the ordered development of material conditions—that is art. (p. 292)

Chapter 7 explores how students' writing can be improved when they sketch a concept map to plan an essay or report. The great advantage of a visual image is that individuals can freely focus on one element, then another, and then take a broader view of how each element relates to the whole. This mimics how humans think. Indeed, students are routinely taught to create an outline before starting to write a paper. Seeing the main points all at once makes it easier for them to create a coherent plan for writing. Yet, creating an outline may not work well for K–5 students, who often write papers on topics about which they are still learning. So, they are unsure what should be the main heading, a subordinate heading, and so forth. A concept map is a more flexible tool because students can start with what they know and add information as they discover it. The visual format allows teachers to use the concept map to check students' understanding and provide immediate feedback.

ENHANCING EXECUTIVE FUNCTION

Executive function (EF) is defined as "an overarching term that refers to mental control processes that enable physical, cognitive, and emotional self-control and are necessary to maintain effective goal-directed behavior" (Corbett et al., 2009, p. 210). Goal-oriented behavior is not only required for academic success but also plays an instrumental role in supporting work and relationships throughout a student's life. Researchers have identified three main components of executive function (Diamond, 2013; Miyake et al., 2000): inhibitory control (the ability to override internal predispositions or external lures), working memory (the capacity to store and retrieve information and work with it), and cognitive flexibility (the ability to ignore distractions, shift perspectives, and adapt to different demands). The development of these processes appears to peak as children start elementary school (Yeager & Yeager, 2013). However, there is evidence that executive function is malleable.

Researchers have found that strategies used in educational arts activities are helpful in strengthening long-term memory. Such activities include rehearsal (repetition), elaboration (extending what is known), enactment (physically acting out a concept or plot), emotional arousal (invoking emotions that help support understanding), and pictorial representation (Rinne et al., 2011). Such techniques may also support executive function development, especially enhancement of working memory and cognitive flexibility. For example, children may be asked (while dancing) to imitate a certain animal or express an emotion as the music plays and also be instructed to assume a particular pose when the music stops. This teaches inhibitory control, because students must repress the urge to start taking the pose while the music is playing; students must also muster the cognitive flexibility to translate verbal instructions into an actual body position. The dance component of the K–2 Teaching Artist Project, described in Chapter 2, contains many such lessons.

ARTS INTEGRATION VERSUS TRANSFER

Throughout this book we have explored the benefits of arts integration, an approach to teaching in which students construct and demonstrate understanding through an art form (Silverstein & Layne, 2010). Yet, researchers diverge in their views of how best to fit the arts into the education of K–5 students. Some scholars argue that the proper way to provide lessons in the arts is not through integrating the visual and performing arts with other subjects but by setting up regular times during the school day when arts lessons are taught by designated arts teachers in traditional arts classrooms (Greene, 2017).

This perspective conflicts with the arts integration approach we have been discussing only when use of arts integration versus specialized arts classes is assumed to be an either–or choice. Having arts specialists teach K–5 students how to play the recorder has clear advantages. Just like literacy, mathematics, science, and social studies, the arts deserve their own time during the school day. However, fears have been expressed that if arts instruction is integrated with science, social studies, and language arts, then schools will be tempted to curtail separate arts classes. That advocates of arts programs might worry about budget cuts is understandable. But the manner in which arts integration can support learning across the K–5 curriculum cannot be reduced to a budgetary argument.

For example, Jay P. Greene (2017) made the following claim in favor of isolating arts education. However, his argument misrepresents how young children learn:

> It is pedagogically unsound to integrate all disciplines, especially when teaching young children, because it demands that students combine knowledge they do not yet possess. Students cannot gain new insights from the connections between geometry and the arts until they first have some mastery of those subjects.

Long before they begin to talk, young children experience the world through their senses. Later, they learn to name and understand phenomena they have already become familiar with. This process of learning through experience continues while children attend elementary school. In Chapter 3, we observed what happened when a school combined an astronomy lesson with a creative movement. Grasping the relationship between Earth's rotation and the time of day can be difficult for 3rd-graders. Yet, when they pretended to be the Earth rotating slowly in a counterclockwise direction, they quickly realized that they could only see the construction-paper sun when facing in its direction. The teacher explained that when they directly faced the sun, it was noon; when they faced directly away from the sun, it was midnight. As the children continued to rotate past midnight, they began to see the sun out of the corner of their eye. It was dawn. This concrete, sensory experience enabled children to envision the effect of Earth's rotation and its relationship to the time of day.

Such symbolic experiences give children an initial handle on complex phenomena, which they will come to understand in more detail later. Adult perceptions of the academic disciplines as intellectual silos, each with its own traditions and conceptual underpinnings, should not be allowed to deprive K–5 students of the sensory experiences they crave; for it is these "Aha!" moments of discovery that help fuel a lifelong love of learning. For students who are still concrete thinkers, sensory experience remains the doorway to understanding. Like mathematics, the arts are both rigorous disciplines in their own right and practical tools that people use every day to gain a better understanding of the world around them.

Transfer

There is evidence that traditional visual and performing arts classes can, in some cases, improve student achievement in other academic disciplines. This phenomenon, known as transfer, is defined as the process and extent to which past experiences affect learning and performance in a new situation. In 2013, the Organisation for Economic Cooperation and Development (best known to educators for PISA, its triennial Programme for International Student Assessment) published *Art for Art's Sake: The Impact of Arts Education* (Winner, Goldstein, & Vincent-Lancrin, 2013). This report examined empirical knowledge about the impact of arts education on other educational outcomes. Only two of the four arts disciplines—music and theater—were found to have had a direct impact on student academic performance, with music instruction benefiting overall academic performance and the study of theater boosting oral language.

Scholars have not completely explained the mechanism by which past experiences (in this case, visual and performing arts lessons) affect student performance in "new situations" or other content areas. However, a contributing factor might be the self-discipline and enhanced sensory awareness that sustained study of music fosters. Similarly, classroom drama focuses on the target skill of oral language. Such discussions make tantalizing topics for exploration. Yet their relevance to arts integration in the schools lies in the use of such research to indicate which arts disciplines may combine well with other content areas. For instance, the K–2 Teaching Artist Project described in Chapter 2 was inspired by prior research showing that classroom drama enhanced oral language skills. While clear experimental evidence of transfer may be lacking for visual art and dance, such research is in its infancy and evidence of synergy may be found.

Integration

In contrast, arts integration in the schools relies on direct instruction by teachers, taking advantage of areas of overlap between an arts lesson and another discipline, without assuming that students will make the connection on their own. Educators guide children to apply arts skills to another content area.

The children are at an age when they love to explore and to be active. Sitting for long periods can cause fidgeting. The tactile, concrete nature of the visual and performing arts not only helps students represent complex concepts to themselves, but also allows them—for a few minutes—to step outside the culture of compliance created by continuing pressure to prepare for standardized tests. During the moments when they are free to experiment, students perk up, newly motivated to invest fresh effort in learning.

References

Adolph, K. E., & Berger, S. A. (2006). Motor development. In W. Damon & R. Lerner (Series eds.) and D. Kuhn & R. S. Siegler (Vol. eds.), *Handbook of child psychology: Volume 2: Cognition, perception, and language* (6th ed., pp. 161–213). New York, NY: Wiley.

Ainsworth, S., Prain, V., & Tytler, R. (2011, August 26). Drawing to learn in science. *Science, 333*(6046), 1096–1097.

Aron, A. R., Fletcher, P. C., Bullmore, E. T., Sahakian, B. J., & Robbins, T. W. (2003). Stop-signal inhibition disrupted by damage to right inferior frontal gyrus in humans. *Nature Neuroscience, 6*(2), 115.

August, D., & Shanahan, T. (Eds.). (2006). *Developing literacy in second-language learners: Report of the national literacy panel on language-minority children and youth.* Mahwah, NJ: Lawrence Erlbaum Associates.

Baddeley, A. D., & Hitch, G. J. (1994). Developments in the concept of working memory. *Neuropsychology, 8*(4), 485–493. doi:10.1037/0894-4105.8.4.485

Barnett, W. S., Jung, K., Yarosz, D. J., Thomas, J., Hornbeck, A., Stechuk, R., & Burns, S. (2008). Educational effects of the Tools of the Mind curriculum: A randomized trial. *Early Childhood Research Quarterly, 23*(3), 299–313. doi:10.1016/j.ecresq.2008.03.001.

Bassok, D., Latham, S., & Rorem, A. (2016). Is kindergarten the new first grade? *AREA Open. 1*(4), 1–31.

Beane, J. A. (1997). *Curriculum integration: Designing the core of democratic education.* New York, NY: Teachers College Press.

Bellamy, G. T., Crawford, L., Marshall, L. H., & Coulter, G. A. (2005, August 1). The fail-safe schools challenge: Leadership possibilities from high reliability organizations. *Educational Administration Quarterly, 41*(3), 383–412.

Bereiter, C., & Scardamalia, M. (1982). From conversation to composition: The role of instruction in a development process. In R. Glazer (Ed.), *Advances in instructional psychology* (Vol. 2, pp. 1–67). Hillsdale, NJ: Lawrence Erlbaum Associates.

Bereiter, C., & Scardamalia, M. (1987). *The psychology of written composition.* Hillsdale, NJ: Lawrence Erlbaum Associates.

Bialystok, E., & DePape, A. M. (2009, April). Musical expertise, bilingualism, and executive functioning. *Journal of Experimental Psychology: Human Perception and Performance, 35*(2), 565–574. doi:10.1037/a0012735

Bierman, K. L., Nix, R. L., Greenberg, M. T., Blair, C., & Domitrovich, C. E. (2008). Executive functions and school readiness intervention: Impact, moderation, and mediation in the Head Start REDI program. *Development and Psychopathology*, *20*(3), 821–843. doi:10.1017/S0954579408000394

Blair, C., Granger, D. A., Willoughby, M., Mills-Koonce, R., Cox, M., Greenberg, M. T., . . . the FLP investigators. (2011, November–December). Salivary cortisol mediates effects of poverty and parenting on executive functions in early childhood. *Child Development*, *82*(6), 1970–1984. doi:10.1111/j.1467-8624.2011.01643.x

Blair, C., & Raver, C. C. (2015). School readiness and self-regulation: A developmental psychobiological approach. *Annual Review of Psychology*, *66th annual review*, 711–731. doi:10.1146/annurev-psych-010814-015221

Blair, C., & Razza, R. P. (2007, March–April). Relating effortful control, executive function, and false belief understanding to emerging math and literacy ability in kindergarten. *Child Development*, *78*(2), 647–663.

Bodrova, E., & Leong, D. J. (2007). *Tools of the mind: The Vygotskyian approach to early childhood education* (2nd ed.). Upper Saddle River, NJ: Pearson.

Bodrova, E., & Leong, D. J. (2015). Vygotskian and post-Vygotskian views on children's play. *American Journal of Play*, *7*(3), 371–388.

Bolton, S., & Hattie, J. (2017). Cognitive and brain development: Executive function, Piaget, and the prefrontal cortex. *Archives of Psychology*, *1*(3).

Booker, C. (2004). *The seven basic plots: Why we tell stories*. London, UK: Continuum.

Britton, J. (1982). *Prospect and retrospect: Selected essays of James Britton*. G. Pradl (Ed.). London, UK: Heinemann.

Brouillette, L. (1997, Spring). Using student writing to create a language of possibility: A study of an inner city writer-in-residence program. *TABOO: The Journal of Culture and Education*, *3*(1).

Brouillette, L. (2010). How the arts help children to create healthy social scripts: Exploring the perceptions of elementary teachers. *Arts Education Policy Review 111*(1), 16–24.

Brouillette, L., Childress-Evans, K., Hinga, B., & Farkas, G. (2014). Increasing the school engagement and oral language skills of ELLs through arts integration in the primary grades. *Journal for Learning through the Arts*, *10*(1). Retrieved from https://escholarship.org/uc/item/8573z1fm

Brouillette, L., & Jennings, L. (2010). Helping children cross cultural boundaries in the borderlands: Arts program at Freese Elementary creates cultural bridges. *Journal for Learning through the Arts 6*(1). Retrieved from http://escholarship.org/uc/item/1kf6p9th

Bruer, J. T. (1993). *Schools for thought: A science of learning in the classroom*. Cambridge, MA: MIT Press.

Bryk, A. S., Gomez, L. M., Grunow, A., & LeMahieu, P. G. (2015). *Learning to improve: How America's schools can get better at getting better*. Cambridge, MA: Harvard Education Press.

Bureau of Labor Statistics. (2017). American time use survey. Retrieved from https://www.bls.gov/tus/

Burnett, F. H. (1905). *A little princess: Being the whole story of Sara Crewe now being told for the first time*. New York, NY: Charles Scribner's Sons.

Carlson, S. M., Mandell, D. J., & Williams, L. (2004). Executive function and theory of mind: Stability and prediction from ages 2 to 3. *Developmental Psychology, 40*(6), 1105–1122. doi:10.1037/0012-1649.40.6.1105

Cassano, D. M. (2014, August 7). Inspire thoughtful creative writing through art. *Edutopia*. Retrieved from https://www.edutopia.org/blog/thoughtful-creative-writing-through-art-denise-cassano

Chall, J. S., & Jacobs, V. A. (2003, Spring). The classic study on poor children's fourth-grade slump. *American Educator, 27*(1). Retrieved from http://www.aft.org/newspubs/periodicals/ae/spring2003/hirschsbclassic.cfm

Chall, J. S., Jacobs, V. A., & Baldwin, L. E. (1990). *The reading crisis: Why poor children fall behind*. Cambridge, MA: Harvard University Press.

Cherry, L. (2002). *A river ran wild*. New York, NY: Harcort.

Clarke, A. C. (1973). *Profiles of the future: An inquiry into the limits of the possible*. London, UK: Phoenix.

Cooper, P. M. (2005). Literacy learning and pedagogical purpose in Vivian Paley's "storytelling curriculum." *Journal of Early Childhood Literacy 5*(3), 229–251.

Corbett, B. A., Constantine, L. J., Hendren, R., Rocke, D., & Ozonoff, S. (2009, April 30). Examining executive functioning in children with autism spectrum disorder, attention deficit hyperactivity disorder and typical development. *Psychiatry Research, 166*(2–3), 210–222. doi:10.1016/j.psychres.2008.02.005

Cronmiller, S. (2007). Essential poetry: Activating the imagination in the elementary classroom. *Journal for Learning through the Arts, 3*(1). Retrieved from https://escholarship.org/uc/item/14q2f3md

Davis, J. (1996). *The MUSE book and guide*. Cambridge, MA: Harvard Graduate School of Education.

Degé, F., Kubicek, C., & Schwarzer, G. (2011, December). Music lessons and intelligence: A relation mediated by executive functions. *Music Perception: An Interdisciplinary Journal, 29*(2), 195–201. doi:10.1525/mp.2011.29.2.195

Denton, P. H. (2002, Spring). What could be wrong with Harry Potter? *Journal of Youth Services in Libraries, 15*(3), 28–32.

DeTemple, J. M., & Tabors, P. O. (1996, August). Children's story retelling as a predictor of early reading achievement. Paper presented at the Biennial Meeting of the International Society for the Study of Behavioral Development, Quebec City, Quebec, Canada. Retrieved from https://eric.ed.gov/?id=ED403543

Dewey, J. (1934). *Art as experience*. New York, NY: Minton, Balch & Company.

Dewey, J. (1977). *The middle works, 1899–1924, Volume 3*. J. A. Boydston (Ed.). Carbondale, IL: Southern Illinois University Press.

Diamond, A. (2012, October). Activities and programs that improve children's executive functions. *Current Directions in Psychological Science, 21*(5), 335–341.

Diamond, A. (2013, January). Executive functions. *Annual Review of Psychology, 64*, 135–168. doi:10.1146/annurev-psych-113011-143750

Diamond, A., Barnett, W. S., Thomas, J., & Munro, S. (2007, November 30). Preschool program improves cognitive control. *Science, 318*(5855), 1387.

Diamond, A., & Lee, K. (2011, August 19). Interventions shown to aid executive function development in children 4 to 12 years old. *Science, 333*(6045), 959–964. doi:10.1126/science.1204529

Duchouquette, C., Loschert, K., & Barth, P. (2014). *Beyond fiction: The importance of reading for information*. Center for Public Education. Retrieved from https://cdn-files.nsba.org/s3fs-public/Beyond-Fiction-Full-Report-PDF.pdf

Dyson, A. H., & Freedman, S. W. (2003). Writing. In J. Flood, D. Lapp, J. R. Squire, & J. M. Jensen (Eds.), *Handbook of research on teaching the English language arts* (2nd ed., pp. 967–992). Mahwah, NJ: Lawrence Erlbaum Associates.

Egan, K. (1997). *The educated mind: How cognitive tools shape our understanding*. Chicago, IL: University of Chicago Press.

Eisner, E. (1998). *The kind of schools we need: Personal essays*. Portsmouth, NH: Heinemann.

Eisner, E. W. (1982). *Cognition and curriculum: A basis for deciding what to teach*. New York, NY: Addison-Wesley Longman.

Eisner, E. W. (1993). Why standards may not improve schools. *Educational Leadership, 50*(5), 22–23.

Eisner, E. W. (2002). *The arts and the creation of mind*. New Haven, CT: Yale University Press.

Eisner, E. W. (2016). *10 lessons the arts teach*. Alexandria, VA: National Art Education Association. Retrieved from https://www.arteducators.org/advocacy/articles/116-10-lessons-the-arts-teach

Elfers, A. M., & Stritikus, T. (2013). How school and district leaders support classroom teachers' work with English language learners. *Educational Administration Quarterly*. doi:10.1177/0013161X13492797

Elmore, R. F. (2000). *Building a new structure for school leadership*. Washington, DC: Albert Shanker Institute.

Essley, R., Rief, L., & Rocci, A. L. (2008). *Visual tools for differentiating reading and writing instruction: Strategies to help students make abstract ideas concrete & accessible*. New York, NY: Scholastic.

Evangelista, B. (2009, November 15). Attention loss feared as high-tech rewires brain. *San Francisco Chronicle*. Retrieved from https://www.sfgate.com/business/article/Attention-loss-feared-as-high-tech-rewires-brain-3281030.php

Fine, B. (1952, October 5). Einstein stresses critical thinking, opposing early specialties. *The New York Times*, p. 37.

Forbes, E. (2011). *Johnny Tremain*. Boston, MA: Houghton Mifflin Harcourt. (Original work published 1943)

Foster, B. (2005, January). Einstein and his love of music. *Physics World, 18*(1).

Frydman, J. S. (2016). Role theory and executive functioning: Constructing cooperative paradigms of drama therapy and cognitive neuropsychology. *The Arts in Psychotherapy, 47*, 41–47.

Gara, T., Brouillette, L., & Farkas, G. (2018). Did the frequency of early elementary classroom arts instruction decrease during the No Child Left Behind era? If so, for whom? *Early Childhood Research Quarterly, 45*, 263–276.

Gazzaniga, M. S. (2008). *Arts and cognition monograph: Summary*. New York, NY: The Dana Foundation.

Geisert, B., & Geisert, A. (1998). *Prairie town*. New York, NY: HMH Books for Young Readers.

Geisert, B., & Geisert, A. (1999). *River town*. New York, NY: HMH Books for Young Readers.

Geisert, B., & Geisert, A. (2000). *Mountain town*. New York, NY: HMH Books for Young Readers.

Geisert, B., & Geisert, A. (2001). *Desert town*. New York, NY: HMH Books for Young Readers.

Getty Museum. (2015). Developing Common Core Habits. Retrieved from https://www.youtube.com/watch?v=__DBkZhyZ3A

Glenberg, A. M. (2010, April 8). Embodiment as a unifying perspective for psychology. *Wiley Interdisciplinary Reviews: Cognitive Science*, *1*(4), 586–596. doi:10.1002/wcs.55

Graff-Radford, J. (2018). How can music help people who have Alzheimer's disease? Retrieved from https://www.mayoclinic.org/diseases-conditions/alzheimers-disease/expert-answers/music-and-alzheimers/faq-20058173

Graham, N. J., & Brouillette, L. (2016). Using arts integration to make science learning memorable in the upper elementary grades: A quasi-experimental study. *Journal for Learning through the Arts*, *12*(1). Retriever from escholarship.org/uc/item/9x61c7kf

Graue, E. (2009). Reimagining kindergarten: Restoring a developmental approach when accountability demands are pushing formal instruction on the youngest learners. *The School Administrator 10*(66), 10–15.

Greene, J. P. (2017). Arts integration is a sucker's game. *Education Week*, *37*(7), 23.

Greene, M. (1977), Toward wide-awakeness: An argument for the arts and humanities in Education. *Teachers College Record*, *79*(1), 119–125.

Greene, M. (2001). *Variations on a blue guitar: The Lincoln Center Institute lectures on aesthetic education*. New York, NY: Teachers College Press.

Greenfader, C. M., & Brouillette, L. (2013, November). Boosting language skills of ELLs through dramatization and movement. *The Reading Teacher*, *67*(3), 171–180. doi:10.1002/TRTR.1192

Greenfader, C. M., & Brouillette, L. (2017). The arts, the common core, and English language development in the primary grades. *Teachers College Record*, *119*(9). http://www.tcrecord.org/library ID Number: 21915

Greenfader, C. M., Brouillette, L., & Farkas, G. (2015, April–June). Effect of a performing arts program on the oral language skills of young English learners. *Reading Research Quarterly*, *50*(2), 185–203. doi:10.1002/rrq.90

Handwerk, B. (2003, June 6). "Songcatchers" document world music. *National Geographic News*.

Harris, P. L. (2000). *The work of the imagination*. Oxford, UK: Blackwell Publishers.

Harvard-Smithsonian Center for Astrophysics, Science Education Department. (1987). *A private universe*. [Video]. Cambridge, MA: Science Media Group.

Hayes, J. R., & Flower, L. S. (2016). Identifying the organization of the writing processes. In L. W. Gregg & E. R. Steinberg (Eds.), *Cognitive processes in writing* (pp. 3–30). New York, NY: Routledge.

Heim, J. (2016, December 6). On the world stage, U.S. students fall behind. *The Washington Post*. Retrieved from https://www.washingtonpost.com/local/education/on-the-world-stage-us-students-fall-behind/2016/12/05/610e1e10-b740-11e6-a677-b608fbb3aaf6_story.html?

Hetland, L., & Winner, E. (2004). Cognitive transfer from arts education to non-arts outcomes: Research evidence and policy implications. In E. Eisner &

M. Day (Eds.), *Handbook on research and policy in art education.* Mahwah, NJ: Lawrence Erlbaum Associates.

Hope, G. (2008). *Thinking and learning through drawing in primary classrooms.* London, UK: Sage.

Hughes, C. (2011, May–June). Changes and challenges in 20 years of research into the development of executive functions. *Infant and Child Development, 20*(3), 251–271.

Inhelder, B., & Piaget, J. (1958). An essay on the construction of formal operational structures. *The growth of logical thinking from childhood to adolescence* (A. Parsons & S. Milgram, Trans.). New York, NY: Basic Looks Good.

International Reading Association & National Council of Teachers of English. (1996). *Standards for the English language art.* Urbana, IL, & Newark, NJ: NCTE/IRA.

Jenkins, J. M., & Astington, J. W. (2000). Theory of mind and social behavior: Causal models tested in a longitudinal study. *Merrill-Palmer Quarterly, 46*(2), 203–220.

Kagan, S. L., Moore, E., & Bredekamp, S. (1995). *Reconsidering children's early development and learning: Toward common views and vocabulary.* Washington, DC: National Education Goals Panel.

Kaku, M. (2017). Albert Einstein. *Encyclopedia Britannica.* Retrieved from https://www.britannica.com/biography/Albert-Einstein

King, S. (2000, July 23). Wild about Harry. *The New York Times.* Retrieved from http://www.nytimes.com/books/00/07/23/reviews/000723.23kinglt.html

Kirsch, I. S., Jungeblut, A., Jenkins, L., & Kolstad, A. (1993). *Adult literacy in America: A first look at the findings of the national adult literacy survey.* Washington, DC: National Center for Education Studies.

Knapp, N. F. (2003). In defense of Harry Potter: An apologia. *School Libraries Worldwide, 9*(1), 78–91.

Koretz, D. (2017). *The testing charade: Pretending to make schools better.* Chicago, IL: University of Chicago Press.

Koziol, L. F., Budding, D. E., & Chidekel, D. (2012). From movement to thought: Executive function, embodied cognition, and the cerebellum. *The Cerebellum, 11*(2), 505–525. doi:10.1007/s12311-011-0321-y

Kress, G. (2009). Assessment in the perspective of a social semiotic theory of multimodal teaching and learning. In C. Wyatt-Smith & J. J. Cumming (Eds.), *Educational assessment in the 21st century: Connecting theory and practice* (pp. 19–41). Dordrecht, The Netherlands: Springer. doi:10.1007/978-1-4020-9964-9_2

Kress, G., & van Leeuwen, T. (2001). *Multimodal discourse: The modes and media of contemporary communication.* New York, NY: Oxford University Press.

Kress, G., & van Leeuwen, T. (2006). *Reading images: The grammar of visual design* (2nd ed.). London, UK: Routledge.

Lawson, R. (1988). *Ben and me: An astonishing life of Benjamin Franklin by his good mouse Amos.* Columbus, GA: Little, Brown Books for Young Readers. (Original work published 1939)

Levitin, D. (2008). *The world in six songs: How the musical brain created human nature.* New York, NY: Dutton.

Longhenry, S. (2005, March). Thinking through art at the Boston Museum of Fine Arts. *SchoolArts Magazine*, *104*(7), 56.

MacIntyre, A. (1981). *After virtue: A study in moral theory*. Notre Dame, IN: University of Notre Dame Press.

Mages, W. K. (2006). Drama and imagination: A cognitive theory of drama's effect on narrative comprehension and narrative production. *Research in Drama Education*, *11*(3), 329–340.

Mages, W. K. (2017). Drama-based interventions and narrative. In N. Kucirkova, C. E. Snow, V. Grøver, & C. McBride (Eds.), *The Routledge international handbook of early literacy education: A contemporary guide to literacy teaching and interventions in a global context* (pp. 296–307). New York, NY: Routledge.

Mah, A. Y. (1999). *Chinese Cinderella: The true story of an unwanted daughter*. New York, NY: Delacorte Press.

Mannes, E. (2011). *The power of music: Pioneering discoveries in the new science of song*. New York, NY: Walker Books.

McCarthy, K. F., Ondaatje, E. H., Zakaras, L., & Brooks, A. (2004). *Gifts of the Muse: Reframing the debate about the benefits of the arts*. Santa Monica, CA: RAND Corporation.

McClelland, M. M., Cameron, C. E., Wanless, S. B., & Murray, A. (2007). Executive function, behavioral self-regulation, and social-emotional competence. In O. N. Saracho & B. Spodek (Eds.), *Contemporary perspectives on social learning in early childhood education* (pp. 83–108). Charlotte, NC: Information Age Publishing.

McLaughlin, M., Glaab, L., & Carrasco, I. H. (2014). *Implementing Common Core State Standards in California: A report from the field*. Stanford, CA: Policy Analysis for California Education.

Mithen, S. (2005). *The singing neanderthals: The origins of music, language, mind and body*. London, UK: Weidenfield & Nicholson.

Mithen, S., Morley, I., Wray, A., Tallerman, M., & Gamble, C. (2006, January 26). The singing Neanderthals: The origins of music, language, mind and body. *Cambridge Archaeological Journal 16*(1), 97–112. doi:10.1017/S0959774306000060

Miyake, A., Friedman, N. P., Emerson, M. J., Witzki, A. H., Howerter, A., & Wager, T. D. (2000, August). The unity and diversity of executive functions and their contributions to complex "frontal lobe" tasks: A latent variable analysis. *Cognitive Psychology*, *41*(1), 49–100. doi:10.1006/cogp.1999.0734

Moreno, S. (2009, December). Can music influence language and cognition? *Contemporary Music Review*, *28*(3), 329–345. doi:10.1080/07494460903404410

Moreno, S., Bialystok, E., Barac, R., Schellenberg, E. G., Cepeda, N. J., & Chau, T. (2011). Short-term music training enhances verbal intelligence and executive function. *Psychological Science*, *22*(11), 1425–1433. doi:10.1177/0956797611416999

Moses, L. (2013). Viewing as a cultural tool in the construction of meaning with expository texts for young bilinguals. *Journal of Language & Literacy Education*, *9*(2), 72–93.

Müller, U., Jacques, S., Brocki, K., & Zelazo, P. D. (2009). The executive functions of language in preschool children. In A. Winsler, C. Fernyhough, & I. Montero (Eds.), Private speech, executive functioning, and the development of verbal self-regulation (pp. 53–68). New York, NY: Cambridge University Press. doi.org/10.1017/CBO9780511581533.005

National Assessment of Academic Progress. (2015). Retrieved from nces.ed.gov/pubsearch/pubsinfo.asp?pubid=2015112

National Center for Education Statistics (NCES). (2018). English Language Learners in Public Schools. Retrieved from nces.ed.gov/programs/coe/indicator_cgf.asp

National Center for Education Statistics (NCES). (2017). U.S. position slips on international reading assessment as other countries improve. [Press release]. Retrieved from www.businesswire.com/news/home/20171205005543/en/U.S.-Position-Slips-International-Reading-Assessment-Countries

National Council for the Social Studies. (1994). *National curriculum standards for social studies: A framework for teaching, learning, and assessment* (executive summary). Silver Springs, MD: National Curriculum Standards for Social Studies. Retrieved from www.socialstudies.org/standards/execsummary

National Education Association. (2008). *English language learners face unique challenges.* Retrieved from http://www.nea.org/assets/docs/HE/ELL_Policy_Brief_Fall_08_(2).pdf

National Governor's Association (2013). *A governor's guide to early literacy: Getting all students reading by third grade.* Washington, DC: National Governor's Association.

National Governors Association Center for Best Practices. (2015). *Common Core State Standards: Development process, 2015.* Washington, DC. Retrieved from www.corestandards.org/about-the-standards/development-process/

National Research Council. (2012). *A Framework for K–12 science education: Practices, crosscutting concepts, and core ideas.* Washington, DC: The National Academies Press.

National Research Council. (2013). *Next generation science standards: For states, by states.* Washington, DC: National Academies Press. Retrieved from https://www.nap.edu/catalog/18290/next-generation-science-standards-for-states-by-states

NORC at the University of Chicago. (2016, April 22). Americans believe civility is on decline. *Science Daily.* Retrieved from http://www.apnorc.org/PDFs/Rudeness/APNORC%20Rude%20Behavior%20Report%20%20PRESS%20RELEASE.pdf

Novak, J. D., & Cañas, A. J. (November 2006). *The theory underlying concept maps and how to construct and use them.* Pensacola, FL: Institute for Human and Machine Cognition. Retrieved from cmap.ihmc.us/Publications/ResearchPapers/TheoryUnderlyingConceptMaps.pdf

O'Donnell, C. L. (2008). Defining, conceptualizing, and measuring fidelity of implementation and its relationship to outcomes in K–12 curriculum intervention research. *Review of Educational Research, 78*(1), 33–84.

O'Keefe, P. A., Ben-Eliyahu, A., & Linnenbrink-Garcia, L. (2013). Shaping achievement goal orientations in a mastery-structured environment and concomitant changes in related contingencies of self-worth. *Motivation and Emotion, 37,* 50–64.

Olshansky, B. (2008). *The power of pictures: Creating pathways to literacy through art, grades K–6*. San Francisco, CA: Jossey-Bass.

Organisation for Economic Cooperation and Development (OECD). (2013). *Outlook 2013: First results from the survey of adult skills*. Paris, France: Organisation for Economic Cooperation and Development. doi.org/10.1787/9789264204256-en

Organisation for Economic Cooperation and Development (OECD). (2016). *Programme for international student assessment (PISA) results from PISA 2015: United Kingdom*. Retrieved from http://www.oecd.org/pisa/pisa-2015-United-Kingdom.pdf

Paris, A. H., & Paris, S. G. (2003, January–March). Assessing narrative comprehension in young children. *Reading Research Quarterly, 38*(1), 36–76. http://dx.doi.org/10.1598/RRQ.38.1.3

Parsons, M. J. (1992). Cognition as interpretation art education. In B. Reimer & R. A. Smith (Eds.), *The arts, education, and aesthetic knowing: Ninety-first yearbook of the national society the study of education* (part 2). Chicago, IL: University of Chicago Press.

Pérez, A. I. (2009) *My diary from here to there*. San Francisco, CA: Children's Book Press.

Pew Research Center. (2018, May 31). Teens, social media & technology 2018. Retrieved from https://www.pewinternet.org/2018/05/31/teens-social-media-technology-2018/

Pew Research Center. (2016, October 6). *The state of American jobs. How the shifting economic landscape is reshaping work and society and affecting the way people think about the skills and training they need to get ahead*. Washington, DC: Pew Research Center. Retrieved from http://www.pewsocialtrends.org/2016/10/06/the-state-of-american-jobs/

Piaget, J. (1954). *The construction of reality in the child* (M. Cook, Trans.). New York, NY: Basic Books.

Piaget, J. (1962). *Play, dreams, and imitation in childhood*. New York, NY: W. W. Norton & Company.

Pinker, S. (1997). *How the mnd works*. New York, NY: W. W. Norton & Company.

President's Committee on the Arts and the Humanities (PCAH). (2011). *Reinvesting in arts education: winning America's future through creative schools*. Washington, DC: Author.

Rauscher, F. H., Shaw, G. L., Levine, L. J., Wright, E. L., Dennis, W. R., & Newcomb, R. L. (1997, February). Music training causes long-term enhancement of preschool children's spatial–temporal reasoning. *Neurological Research, 19*(1), 2–8.

Ray, K. W. (2010). *In pictures and in words: Teaching the qualities of good writing through illustration study*. Portsmouth, NH: Heinemann.

Rinne, L., Gregory, E., Yarmolinskaya, J., & Hardiman, M. (2011). Why arts integration improves long-term retention of content. *Mind, Brain, and Education, 5*(2), 89–96. doi:10.1111/j.1751-228X.2011.01114.x

Robb, L. (2011). The myth of learn to read/read to learn. *Scholastic Teacher*. Retrieved from http://www.scholastic.com/teachers/article/myth-learn-read-read-learn

Robertson, K. (2006). Visual thinking strategies for improved comprehension. *Colorín Colorado*. Retrieved from www.colorincolorado.org/article/visual-thinking-strategies-improved-comprehension

Rowling, J. K. (1997). *Harry Potter and the philosopher's stone*. London, UK: Bloomsbury.

Rowling, J. K. (2000). *Harry Potter and the goblet of fire*. New York, NY: Scholastic Press.

Russell, J. (2011). From child's garden to academic press: The role of shifting institutional logics in redefining kindergarten education. *American Education Research Journal, 48*(2), 236–67.

Samson J. F., & Lesaux, N. (2015). Disadvantages language minority students and their teachers: a national picture. *Teachers College Record 117*(2), 1–26.

Sawhill, I., & Rodrigue, E. (2015). *The three norms analysis: Technical background*. Washington, DC: Brookings.

Schellenberg, E. G. (2004). Music lessons enhance IQ. *Psychological Science, 15*(8), 511–514. doi:10.1111/j.0956-7976.2004.00711.x

Schellenberg, E. G., & Moreno, S. (2010). Music lessons, pitch processing, and g. *Psychology of Music, 38*(2), 209–221. doi.org/10.1177/0305735609339473

Schneider, Donald; and others. (1994). *Expectations of excellence: Curriculum standards for social studies* (Bulletin 89). Washington, DC: National Council for the Social Studies.

Schwartz, D. L., Bransford, J. D., and Sears, D. (2005). Efficiency and innovation in transfer. In Mestre, J. (Ed.), *Transfer of learning: Research and perspectives.* Greenwich, CT: Information Age Publishing.

Schutz, A. (1967). *The phenomenology of the social world*. Evanston, IL: Northwestern University Press.

Segal, D. (2017, July 1). That diss song known as "Yankee Doodle." *The New York Times*. Retrieved from https://www.nytimes.com/2017/07/01/sunday-review/that-diss-song-known-as-yankee-doodle.html

Shams, L., & Seitz, A. R. (2008, November 1). Benefits of multisensory learning. *Trends in Cognitive Sciences, 12*(11), 411–417. doi:10.1016/j.tics.2008.07.006

Siegel, D. J. (2012). *The developing mind: How relationships and the brain interact to shape who we are* (2nd ed.). New York, NY: Guilford Press.

Silverstein, L. B., & Layne, S. (2010). *Defining arts integration*. Washington, DC: The John F. Kennedy Center for the Performing Arts. Retrieved from http://www.kennedy-center.org/education/partners/defining_arts_integration.pdf

Simpson, K. (2016, May 4). The importance of storytelling. *Considered*. (The Faculty of Education blog at Canterbury Christ Church University.) Retrieved from http://www.consider-ed.org.uk/the-importance-of-storytelling/

Smagorinsky, P. (2007, January). Vygotsky and the social dynamics of classrooms. *English Journal, 97*(2), 61–66.

Smith, H. (2010). *The effects of a drama-based language intervention on the development of theory of mind and executive function in urban kindergarten children*. (Unpublished doctoral dissertation). Atlanta, GA: Georgia State University.

Smith, M. K., Wood, W. B., Adams, W. K., Wieman, C., Knight, J. K., Guild, N., & Su, T. T. (2009, January 2). Why peer discussion improves student performance on in-class concept questions. *Science, 323*(590), 122–124. doi:10.1126/science.1165919

Smithsonian Institution. (2002). The silk road: Connecting cultures, creating trust. Retrieved from https://festival.si.edu/2002/the-silk-road/nomads-silk-road-stories/smithsonian

Smithsonian Institution. (2013). What are winter counts? Retrieved from wintercounts.si.edu/

Snow, C. (2010, April 23). Academic language and the challenge of reading for learning about science. *Science, 328* (5977), 450–452.

Snow, C. E., & Uccelli, P. (2009). The challenge of academic language. In D. R. Olson & N. Torrance (Eds.), *The Cambridge handbook of literacy* (pp. 112–133). Cambridge, UK: Cambridge University Press.

Tolstoy, L. (1994). *What is art?* (W. Gareth Jones, Trans.). London, UK: Bloomsbury. (Original work published in 1897)

VanSledright, B. (2008). Narratives of Nation-State, Historical Knowledge, and School History Education. *Review of Research in Education, 32*, 109–146. Retrieved from http://www.jstor.org/stable/20185114

Vygotsky, L. S. (1967). Play and its role in the mental development of the child. *Soviet Psychology, 5*(3), 6–18.

Vygotsky, L. S. (1986). *Thought and language*. A. Kozulin (Ed.). Cambridge, MA: MIT Press. (Original work published in 1934)

Walker, E. M., McFadden, L. B., Tabone, C., & Finkelstein, M. (2011). Contribution of drama-based strategies. *Youth Theatre Journal, 25*(1), 3–15. doi:10.1080/08929092.2011.569471

Whitman, W. (2002). *Leaves of grass and other writings*. New York, NY: W. W. Norton & Company.

Wilson, J. Q. (1994, April). Tales of virtue, *Commentary, 97*(4), 30–34.

Winner, E., Goldstein, T., & Vincent-Lancrin, S. (2013). *Art for art's sake? The impact of arts education*. Paris, France: Organisation for Economic Co-operation and Development Publishing. https://doi.org/10.1787/9789264180789-en..

Wolpert-Gawron, H. (2017, February 6). Heroes on a learning adventure. *Edutopia*. Retrieved from www.edutopia.org/blog/heroes-learning-adventure-heather-wolpert-gawron

Wong-Fillmore, S., & Valadez, C. (1985). Teaching bilingual learners. In M. S. Wittrock (Ed.), *Handbook on research on teaching* (pp. 481–519). Washington, DC: American Educational Research Association.

Yeager, M., & Yeager, D. (2013). *Executive function & child development*. New York, NY: W. W. Norton & Company.

Yenawine, P. (2013) *Visual thinking strategies: Using art to deepen learning across school disciplines*. Cambridge, MA: Harvard Education Press.

Index

About the Author

Liane Brouillette is a professor at the School of Education at the University of California, Irvine. Her research interests focus on the use of arts-based strategies to deepen student understanding. Dr. Brouillette's recent articles include "The Arts, the Common Core, and English Language Development in the Primary Grades," published in *Teachers College Record* (2017); "Effect of a Performing Arts Program on the Oral Language Skills of Young English learners," which appeared in *Reading Research Quarterly* (2015); and "Boosting Language Skills of ELLs Through Dramatization and Movement," published in *The Reading Teacher* (2013). She serves as the managing editor of the *Journal for Learning Through the Arts*.